To Marketa
Much love
Peggy. 2010

from Belfast to Belsen and Beyond

Margaret (Peggy) Fink (pictured above with her daughter Michelle in 2002) was born in Belfast, Ireland in 1913 and was thus a young woman when refugees from Nazi Germany began to arrive in Ireland. Seeing the needs of these people she co-founded the Belfast Committee for Refugees form Germany and Austria. After the war was over she again found work serving the needs of refugees and displaced persons, work she continued, together with her husband Egon, for over 40 years.

from Belfast to Belsen and Beyond

My journey through the upheavals of 20th century Europe

Margaret G. Fink

PenFolk Publishing, Blackburn Victoria
December, 2008

Published for Margaret G. Fink and Michelle Fink in December 2008 by

PenFolk Publishing
21 Ronley Street
Blackburn Victoria 3130

National Library of Australia Cataloguing-in-Publication entry:

Author:	*Fink, Margaret Grace, 1913*
Title:	*from Belfast to Belsen and Beyond : my journey through the upheavals of 20th century Europe / Margaret G. Fink; edited by Michelle Fink*
ISBN:	*978 1875894 72 7 (pbk)*
Subjects:	*Fink, Margaret Grace, 1913–*
	Women social reformers—Biography
	Women human rights workers—Biography
	Refugees, Jewish—Europe—History—20th century
	World War, 1939–1945—Refugees
Other Authors/Contributors:	
	Fink, Michelle, 1950–
Dewey Number:	*03.484092*

Design and production by

Bill Ellemor, PenFolk Publishing

Cover design by

Bill Ellemor, PenFolk Publishing

It's giving and doing for somebody else—
on all that, life's splendour depends

Foreword

"There are two types of people in the world now—those who have been in a concentration camp and those who have not."

These are the words of a young Rumanian woman who had been forced to play her cello in an orchestra at the entrance to a gas chamber in one of the Nazis' extermination camps. Her words come down to us through the years because Peggy Fink has remembered them and the young woman who spoke them to her at the Belsen displaced persons' camp after the war was over. When you enter into the world of this memoir, you are refusing forgetfulness—you will meet many people pushed along by the winds of war and its aftermath. At some point in their turbulent lives, they crossed paths with a young woman trying to do her best to be of service to them, and to her times.

Peggy Fink, now in her mid-90s, and living in Cambridge, carries us back to her childhood in Belfast. Born in 1913, Peggy dates her first memories from the end of World War One. A large house for a large cosmopolitan Ulster family, a freethinking father, a loving mother, the warmth and wonders of childhood. As Proust so memorably wrote, after all the years it is the senses that we refuse to relinquish, and so we are given the gift of Peggy's cherished first glimmers of the life around her:

> "A spikey hedgehog rolled in the netting of the shed ... the vision of the evening sun shining on the massive dark red ruins of Kenilworth Castle

against a threatening storm-blue sky ... a few spring days teasing out the primroses and violets and the celandines along the edges of the stream, and the coast road was edged with bushes of flaming gorse and red and purple budding fuchsia."

How do we explain what stays with us, what in the last analysis means life to us? In the pages of this memoir we are given one story of how the human journey takes stock of itself, of what it all seems to have come down to.

We follow this young woman through her early education and work years in Northern Ireland, her experiences in industry, her friendships, the illness of her mother; the firsts she is part of—the founding of nursery schools for poor children in Belfast where children were often sewn into their clothes in winter for warmth, the birth of the study of the social sciences, the beginning of the Girl Guide Movement. And then, in 1937, rumors start reaching Belfast of the terrible plight of refugees from Nazi Germany who were arriving in the UK. Peggy, whom we have come to know as a straightforward young woman who sees what needs to be done and then tries her best to do it, will work with Jewish welfare organizations for the next 40 years.

Her work starts with the Belfast Committee for Refugees from Germany and Austria and she becomes a very active member of a committee dedicated to welcoming the displaced. "I often met these anxious and weary travelers as they got off the boat in the early morning in Belfast, bringing them home for breakfast and helping them get settled for their new life in Ireland." After the declaration of war in 1939, she witnesses the authorities' sometimes arbitrary sorting out of these new arrivals as to who could be trusted and who could not, and helps to organize internment locally for many vulnerable people to avoid their being sent to offshore prisoner of war camps. She joins the Air Raid Defense forces and trains to be an industrial welfare and personnel manager—all new worlds of expertise. We learn of the bombings of Belfast and the generosity of strangers to war-torn civilians.

In 1945, Peggy goes to Europe to join relief units of the American Jewish Joint Distribution Committee, eventually finding herself posted to the liberated Belsen Concentration Camp, where she sets up a procedure to help reunite survivors with families, wherever these still exist. We see through her eyes the complexities of living through liberation only to enter a devastated personal world. Peggy shares her pages with us as she shared her life with people whose courage, spirit and desolation would have gone unmarked if not for her paying attention. People such as Magda, who committed suicide at 19 after liberation because she had no family to return to and no place she could trust to be safe.

During these years of trying to help rebuild a world for desolate refugees, Peggy meets and marries Egon Fink, who had been a member of the French Foreign Legion and the French Resistance, a resourceful and committed freedom fighter who outwitted the Fascist enemy time after time, eventually running a home for refugee children. Together until his death in 1971, the couple continue their work of rescue and reconstruction of Jewish lives devastated by national turmoils. The fifties finds them in Casablanca, now with their young daughter Michelle, trying to aid communities of impoverished Jews scattered throughout Morocco.

These days we speak of globalization, but Peggy Fink crossed boundaries for most of her life in the twentieth century; history and her desire to alleviate human distress forced her to. She followed exiles and found homes, friends, work and pleasures in various parts of Europe and in French-speaking North Africa. She slips easily into French or German, an unpretentious true cosmopolitan.

In these pages lives a distilled chapter of history—memories of childhood scrapes and bony-kneed friends, romances and factory floors, skiing trips in the Alps, beloved friends reuniting in new countries and, above all, a time when war and its effect displaced and left bereft so many. Sadly, concerns with border security, displaced peoples, and national cruelties have followed Peggy and the rest of us into this new century—but perhaps there is reason for hope as long as there are people with the compassion, generosity and straightforward desire to intercede that mark the life of this indomitable woman.

Joan Nestle,
Melbourne, Australia,
2007

Acknowledgements

I wish to acknowledge and thank all of those without whom this project would never have come to fruition.

In particular Christopher Stevens, who was the first to convince Peggy that her story had to be told and started the ball rolling; Kathryn Puffett who spent endless hours word processing the original manuscript and digitizing numerous photographs, as well as proof reading the text with Peggy; many of Peggy's friends who read the original manuscripts and made helpful suggestions, especially Liz Schoenberg who has since passed away. Over the internet I have had support from my dear childhood friend and 'sister' Caroline Handler in Vienna, and my cousins, especially Julia Boyd in the UK. In Melbourne I have had much help from Joan Nestle who has encouraged me by reading the manuscript, seeking out editors and publishers, and writing a thoughtful Foreword.

And finally, I wish to thank Peggy, who has been so patient in waiting for this work to appear.

Michelle Fink,
Melbourne

Prologue

This is the story of my mother who was born Margaret Grace Loewenthal (known as Peggy) on the 9th of April 1913 in Belfast, Northern Ireland. She was the youngest daughter of an assimilated Jewish merchant family of German descent.

Her paternal grandfather, Julius Löwenthal, came to Belfast from Hamburg to become a partner in and later the owner of Moore & Weinberg, linen merchants. In Belfast Julius, who was Jewish, married his landlady's daughter, Jane Rea McCully, who was a strict Presbyterian. He joined her at Elmwood Church, and the children were brought up as Presbyterians. Peggy's father did not agree with the Presbyterians and became a free thinker at the age of fifteen. His daughters were left to make their own decisions about the difficult attitude to religion that prevailed in Northern Ireland and were brought up as neither Jews nor Protestants.

Peggy's father, John McCaldin Loewenthal, was the eldest son and became sole proprietor of Moore & Weinberg when his father died. He was educated at and later became a Governor of the Royal Belfast Academical Institution and was the chairman of the Board of Govenors of Richmond Lodge, a progressive school in Belfast. When he was awarded an honorary degree at Queen's University, Belfast, in 1940 he was described as having a connection with 'almost every progressive movement in the city'.

Her maternal grandfather, Julius Iklé, came from Hamburg but moved to Paris with his family, and this is where her mother Elsa was raised. Julius was one of the 15 children of Moses and Sara Iklé. Moses ran a textile import and export business which had originally been in his wife Sara's family (Joseph and Bella Jonas from Hamburg). Moses' father, Levy Iklé, lived in "auf dem Damm", a suburb of Peine near Hannover. He is thought to be the first of that family to have taken on the name Iklé, in accordance to the laws passed in the kingdom of Westfalen on 31st March 1808 and 4th November 1811, and then in Hannover in 1827 which decreed that Jews had to assume surnames. Prior to that they just added their father's name to their own, e.g. Isaak Levy was the son of Levy Isaak, and his son would again be Isaak Levy. It is said in our family that Iklé is the abbreviation of Isaak Levi, with the accent aigu

Portraits of Elsa Iklé and John Loewenthal on their wedding day, 21 April 1903

in fact being an apostrophe, denoting that this name is an abbreviation. The accent aigu would have been very fashionable during the rule of Napoleon. Julius Iklé and his brothers founded Iklé frères & Co, a large textile import and export business with branches in St Gallen, Paris, New York, Berlin and Vienna. The family was thus dispersed throughout Europe and America.

Peggy's mother, Elsa, had an older brother, Charles (named Carl Felix, but known as Uncle Charlie), who represented Iklé frères & Co in New York. He was born in 1879 and moved to New York around 1903. Charlie was a great art collector and had many artist and musician friends, including Ravel, Prokofiev (to whom he loaned money for the fare from New York to Chicago to attend the first North American performance of his *Love of Three Oranges*), Modigliani and Dufy. He became a patron of the Metropolitan Museum of Art and the Cloisters, leaving important works of art to both when he died.

It is with this background that Peggy entered into life—a life in which she sought out and rose to the challenges of society and history. In her later years, she has entertained and moved more and more people with stories from her life, and they in turn asked her to record her memories in a more permanent way.

These are her recollections.

Peggy: Growing up in Belfast

Early Childhood

I had three sisters, Helen, Amélie and Joan; I was the youngest, born in 1913. My earliest memories are from around the time of the end of the First World War. I lived with my father and my mother, three older sisters, a cook, a housemaid and a nanny in a large house that had belonged to my grandfather, set in a big garden which sloped down a steep daffodil-covered hill to a tennis court at the back. This was surrounded by tall old trees, and under a great chestnut tree at one end was a garden shed filled with musty-smelling netting (which was used to cover gooseberry bushes), a squeaking tennis court marker and garden tools.

Edgar, the gardener, used to make huge bonfires with the fallen leaves in autumn, and in the ashes we baked potatoes till their skins were charcoal black and the inside was fluffy white and delicious. When eating them we got comfortably filthy. One day Edgar found a spiky hedgehog rolled up in the netting in the shed, and we looked at it with great wonder.

Edgar used to keep cigarette cards from his packets of Will's Woodbine 'fags' for me, and my mother was very shocked one day to hear me ask, 'Edgar, do you have a Struggle for Existence?' (She didn't realize that this was a series of cards depicting plants that grew in strange places without much soil or water.)

I remember one spring a fat pigeon found a celluloid pingpong ball lying on the tennis court, which it took to be an egg, and it sat on it for days, trying to hatch it. My friend Ethna Glendinning from next door came with her new Brownie box camera and took a photo of the bird from only a few feet away.

Peggy, c.1915

Lennoxvale
Photograph taken by Robert J. Welsh

We moved into the house at 5 Lennoxvale, which had belonged to my paternal grandfather, Julius Löwenthal, from a smaller one, 'Elboron', at no. 1 Marlborough Park on the corner of the Malone Road, where we four girls were born. I was about three years old at the time. I can dimly remember the move, in a horse-drawn cab, the roof piled high with all sorts of luggage, including my sister Joan's horse tricycle. At the gate, as we drove past the bush of sweet-smelling, white flowering syringa, the trike got caught in its branches, came loose and fell off the cab, breaking a foot off the dappled horse.

Our nursery was a large front room looking out on the drive, with three big bay windows and one other window facing the road. There was a gas fire with a high fireguard around it, and there was a picture over the fireplace of a girl driving white geese. Here Nanny, Joan and I slept in a row—I in a cot, Joan in a little iron bed and Nanny in a brass one. Each had a chamber pot beneath, mine small blue-edged enamel, Joan's and Nanny's old Victorian china with pink roses and blue flowers.

The first night in our new room, in which my father had assured us we could do whatever we liked, we were safely tucked in our beds, Joan with Teddy, Iza the bear (who had springs in his hind legs so that if you hit his rump he would bounce along) and big and little Toby (black stuffed

John Loewenthal and his two youngest daughters in the garden at Lennoxvale, c.1917
Joan on his right, his left arm around Peggy

dogs). Little Toby had a stiff neck because his head had been sewn on again after having come off when he had been washed in hot water to get castor oil off him.

I had taken a small pencil with me into my cot and through the bars on the nice clean pink wall I drew a little stick man in a top hat. My father, coming to say good night, was very cross to see the scribble on the freshly painted wall. But I reminded him that he had said, 'You may do whatever you like in your new nursery', whereupon he left, shutting the door behind him.

I was not as comfortable as I might have been in my cot, as Joan liked to hold my hand when going to sleep, and to reach her through the bars of my cot I had to sleep halfway down it.

In the morning, half asleep, I would climb over the side of my cot and stagger sleepily across Joan's bed to get into Nanny's bed for a 'cuggle'. In her Irish Donegal brogue she called me her 'wee bedfellow'. Then she would get up, and I would sleepily watch her getting dressed under her voluminous nightie, which billowed like a bell tent in a gale.

I think it was about this time that my mother offered to buy me a 'youngbrella' as soon as I stopped wetting my cot at night. Ultimately I did get one, with a beautiful green parrot's head with beady eyes for a handle.

At the end of the day it was upstairs to a bath in the green and white tiled bathroom. Here, lying in delicious warm water, one could look out of the small west window, in summer to a low setting sun and in winter at a starry black sky. Then Nanny would take a big white towel off the warm rail and wrap me up on her knee. A mug of warm milk and a crisp water biscuit buttered and sprinkled with 'window sugar' (preserving sugar) waited for me before I was tucked in to bed.

When I was about five Joan and Amélie developed scarlet fever and had to go off to the isolation hospital in Purdysburn. I watched through the slit of a slightly opened bathroom door (while drinking my mug of milk) the two bundles, Am and Joan, being carried down the stairs to the ambulance.

Next day Nanny and I were sent off to the house of Miss Neill, an old lady in Marlborough Park, while the house was fumigated. Nanny and I slept in a big double bed with a crisp white lace-edged linen bedspread, and we had meals in the kitchen with Sarah, the maid, beside a big black range.

Amélie and Joan were in hospital for eleven weeks—over Christmas. I went with my father to buy them presents in a toyshop and chose for Joan an elegant celluloid swan and for Amélie some tin soldiers.

I still remember celebrating at the end of World War I. My mother cleared the cupboard of the rationing bowls that used to hold the family's sugar ration. During sugar

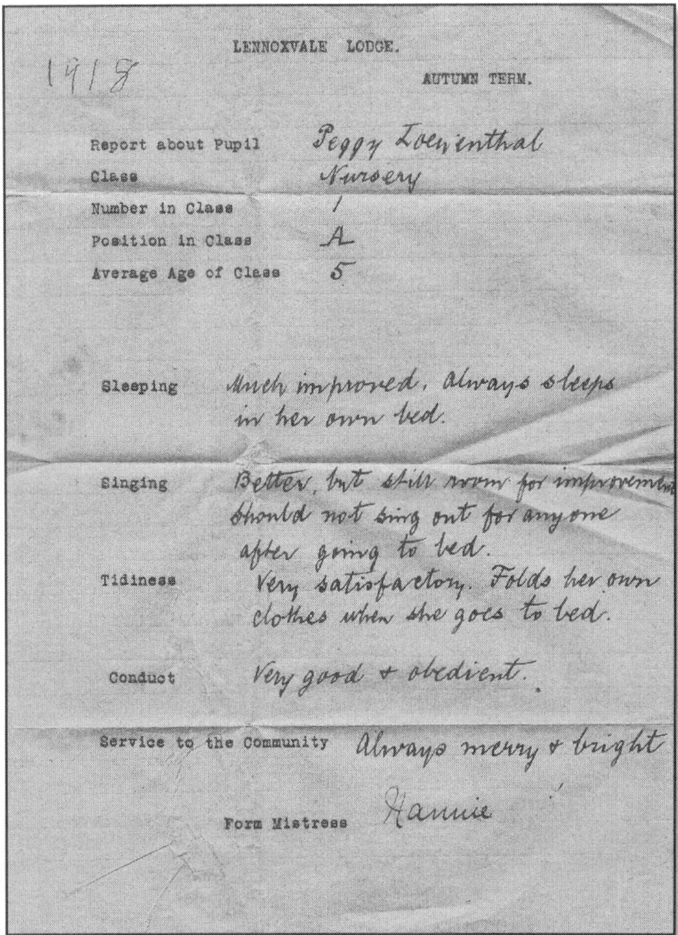

1918

LENNOXVALE LODGE.

AUTUMN TERM.

Report about Pupil Peggy Loewenthal
Class Nursery
Number in Class 1
Position in Class A
Average Age of Class 5

Sleeping Much improved, always sleeps in her own bed.

Singing Better, but still room for improvement. Should not sing out for anyone after going to bed.

Tidiness Very satisfactory. Folds her own clothes when she goes to bed.

Conduct Very good + obedient.

Service to the Community Always merry + bright

Form Mistress Nannie

'Report' issued to Peggy aged 5 by her father— so that she should not feel left out as her older sisters all had school reports

rationing we each gave a little bit of our sugar to our father for his porridge. Everyone got very excited at the armistice, and I turned somersaults round the dining room table to rejoice, not really understanding the significance of the news that the fighting had ended.

Shortly after, my mother was able to phone her sister Amélie in Frankfurt, where she and her family had survived the war years. Aunt Amélie later visited us, and I remember how astonished I was that she ate the skin of her potato. In Germany they had had little food, and nothing edible was thrown away.

Our dear Donegal nanny left us when I was a little older. She went to work for a countess in Paris and wrote to my mother that the count 'was like a roaring lion from Singapore'.

When Joan and Amélie came home from school at the end of term with their reports my father would give each of them half a crown for the good marks they had got. So that I should not be jealous, he would type me a report. It was signed by 'Nanny, Form Mistress' and said 'Peggy now dresses herself, does not wet her bed' etc., and I got half a crown too!

Joan and I still slept together in the nursery, and if the grown-ups had a dinner party we would creep out of our bed to peer downstairs into the hall through the banisters to watch the guests go from the drawing room to the dining room. Should anyone head for the stairs, we would whisper our secret motto—'QQ' (Quick and Quiet!)—and leap back into our beds.

One very friendly cook used to come and say goodnight to us and bring up little handfuls of raisins. My father often had in his 'collar drawer' a box of chocolate dragées, and if we came to see him getting ready to go out to an evening function we would be given a 'chocolate button' from this supply.

I also remember my father one Christmas giving us wonderful wooden guns with paper caps filled with some explosive which made a great bang when one pulled the trigger—and how upset my mother was, as she disapproved strongly of such toys.

Then I had a special birthday. I had seen in the local post office window a huge teddy with which I fell in love, but which I knew it was impossible to have. The evening before my birthday my father walked to the shop after returning from the city office and came back with the big beast under his arm. It was a joyous morning when I got my presents and the teddy was on the table.

Mother used to come into our bedroom in the mornings, saying to Joan that she should not pull up the blinds at 5.30am so that she could see to read her book as 'Wee Pegs needs her sleep'. I was the dormouse and Joan the bookworm.

When the summer holidays came, Mother would wake us very early to start our journey to Ballycastle, where we had the same house each year. We would all pile into the horse-drawn cab to go to the station, trunks and cases

Peggy on the beach at Ballycastle, c.1920

piled on the roof. The 'big' train took us to Ballymoney station, arriving about 9.00am; here the stationmaster welcomed us, and in his office we had breakfast with watery boiled eggs. Then the slow little train, on a single line, would take us through fields of 'retting flax' with a very pungent odour, to Ballycastle. Nanny was still with us, armed for emergencies with a tin potty which was emptied out of the window.

There was a tale told of this little train. When a passenger leant out of the window to ask why the train had stopped, the answer was, 'There's a cow on the line'. Ten minutes later, the train stopped again, and the passenger asked if there was another cow on the line. The reply was, 'No, sir, it's the same cow'.

Our house was on the edge of the shore beside the wooden bridge that crossed the peat-brown river flowing into the sea. Behind stretched the golf links and the sand dunes that edged the coast.

In all weathers we would run down to the beach and bathe in the ever cold Atlantic waves, four little Loewenthal and three Symmers girls, Jessie, Isabel and Paddy, who were friends from Belfast and rented the adjoining house. Back at the house, which was called Glenshesk after the nearby river, we would find mother waiting with cups of hot Bovril to warm us up as she helped to rub us dry. We were blue with cold and had little feeling in our toes, but it was always a great deal of fun.

Our father remained in town to work during the week and joined us at weekends. Then he would fish for trout in the Glenshesk river or in the mountain lakes on Fairhead.

One day while casting across a river pool the fly got caught on the tail of a nearby bullock, with terrible consequences. Another time a swallow took his fly in mid air. But the worst adventure was when his cast hooked the wig of his gillie, Jenkins. (My father tactfully turned his back while Jenkins took the wig off and unhooked the fly.)

Frequently Joan and I would get up very early and look for mushrooms on the golf links stretching out behind the house along the shore. The grass sparkled with dew, and the bright sun shone on the fresh green links and the nearby sand dunes, and if we were lucky we would return with enough mushrooms to fry with the family breakfast of bacon, eggs and potato cakes. Sometimes on our return we would meet Ben the milkman on his early rounds and would get a lift in the horse-drawn cart down the last few yards to the house.

I have many happy memories of summers in Ballycastle: of Blackmores, the vegetable gardens with high stone walls on which one could walk if one was courageous; of the long rows of redcurrant bushes where one could eat while picking; of Lawrence and Boyd, the grocery that sold everything, where we took hours deciding how we would spend our precious sixpence pocket money.

Once I bought a paperback copy of *Black Beauty* from Mr Lawrence and wept so much when reading it in bed that my pillow was soggy.

At the Llamas Fair in August—a very old festival which takes place to this day—the Diamond (market square) was full of stalls, and a small primitive circus appeared in a tent nearby.

Then there were the picnic teas in 'Moat's Bay', a sandy cove behind a jutting brown tongue of rocks at the end of the long beach. Mother's friend Mrs Moat took us there the first time. Here we bathed (without bathing costumes), played in rock pools and collected shells and driftwood to light a fire on which to boil the tea kettle. After our picnic we would trudge home weary, grubby and very content.

One day while we were away our kind fat cook went out to shop, leaving the house empty, and on our return we found a note on the door saying, 'I have gone out. The key is under the mat'!

We had our annual summer holiday in Ballycastle, and at Easter we spent two weeks in Newcastle at the foot of Slieve Donard Mountain on the coast of County Down. The weather was often cool and blustery, but a few spring days teased out the primroses and violets and the celandines along the edges of the stream, and the coast road was edged with bushes of flaming gorse and red and purple budding fuchsia.

Nanny, Peggy, Mother and Joan in Newcastle co Down, c.1914, on a breakwater wall outside the Slieve Donard Hotel

Many years later my sister Joan and her husband Tom rented a tiny cottage on the slopes of the Mourne Mountains above the Bloody Bridge. At that time one could still find quiet solitude in the lovely countryside of Northern Ireland.

School Days

My three sisters and I all went to school at Richmond Lodge in Belfast, and later Helen took herself off to an English boarding school. I remember my first day at the school. I had of course visited the kindergarten when Joan was there and already knew Miss McDonald, the teacher who was known as Miss McD, a wonderful person who also ran the school company of Girl Guides. (The second Belfast company was the first of the Girl Guide movement in Northern Ireland, started in 1914.)

The kindergarten was in a large airy room with small tables and chairs, a 'sand table' (a metal tray table containing sand approx 10cm deep) and a pile of great wooden building blocks in one corner. There was also a large cupboard where each child had a shelf to keep pencil and paper. A few hours after I arrived, a small dark-haired girl came shyly through the door, and I, by now being an 'old girl' who knew all, thought she was a new arrival and wanted to show her where to put her belongings in the big cupboard. But Sylvia had only been delayed and was late in getting to school; she was not at all pleased at being treated as a newcomer.

I was very flattered when two small boys invited me into their fort built of wooden bricks. One, Maurice Gibson (known as Bony because of the knobbly knees on the long legs protruding from his grey flannel shorts), later became an eminent judge and was killed when the IRA blew up his car. The other, Sam Carr, later became a publisher. His brother, Tom Carr, is a 'collectable' painter.

I really did enjoy my eleven years at Richmond Lodge and have many happy memories of my time there, one from the early days, when Sylvia Pring brought her pet white mice to the French class and poor Mademoiselle was terrified and shocked. Sylvia also used to hand round sweets to the class, and I always asked for one for my sister Joan.

At the weekly Wednesday Festival Morning the whole school met for an hour and one class would act, sing, recite poems etc. On one occasion Joan's form were acting a scene from *Julius Caesar*, and the girls were told to bring a sheet to wear as a Roman toga. Joan remembered this only at the last moment before leaving for school and grabbed the first sheet off a pile in the linen cupboard. As it happened, this was the ironing sheet and, to my dismay, she appeared in a toga covered in scorch marks.

It was about this time that Miss Purvis, the head teacher, decided that she would try the Dalton system of education in the senior school. In this method each child was given a contract: a piece of paper which was divided into subjects, with assignments of work in each subject. The contract lasted for three weeks. A classroom was devoted to each subject, and the teacher of that subject sat in a room. The assignment of work was put up on the notice board and you were allowed to choose how you allotted your time. You had to do so many exercises from the relevant book, and if you had any difficulty with this work you could ask the teacher for help. When you had done this assignment you left your book for correction by the teacher, and it was graded—A, A minus and so on—and a blue arrow was written on your contract to say that you had completed that work. When you had finished the three weeks' work for mathematics, and if you enjoyed mathematics and had managed to have free time, you could do supplementary work in this subject and you were then given a red arrow instead of a blue one.

The idea was that you would have the self-discipline to organize your work as you liked. Some people got through the subjects they did not like first. I think I always tackled the maths assignment first, as I enjoyed that much more than literature or the other subjects.

This was quite an adventurous idea for the time. I do not remember how long we continued with the Dalton method. I think it lasted only one or two terms before it was decided that we should go back to the conventional form of teaching, but it was interesting while it lasted.

There was great anxiety over my first public exams—Junior Certificate—which I just managed to pass.

Towards the end of my schooling came the great delight of a week's visit to Stratford upon Avon with some twenty girls from the senior forms and two teachers. In nightly visits to the Shakespeare Theatre we saw five plays, including my first *King Lear.* This visit sparked in me a lifelong interest in the theatre.

We also had splendid visits to Warwick and Kenilworth Castles. The latter was unforgettable for me—the vision of the evening sun shining on the massive dark red ruins against a threatening storm-blue sky is still a picture in my memory. Everything about this trip made a deep and lasting impression on me.

Miss McD lived till she was over eighty, and she told me later how my mother was worried when I started school, as I was slow learning to read and write, but Miss McD assured her that 'Peggy will be all right'. Well, I did manage to pass my Matric, though I had to take a second shot at the English essay and, with a 'masterpiece' on a given subject (Shakespeare and Patriotism), finally got through. One of the other subjects was Pedantry, and one of my school friends wrote an essay about a walking tour!

There were games two afternoons a week. Each Monday and Friday at 1.30pm we would meet at the end of a long lane that led to the playing fields. In summer there was tennis and terribly boring cricket or rounders. The rest of the year we breathlessly played lacrosse. On several occasions there were exciting excursions to Dublin to play rival lacrosse teams, and we stayed with the families of the Dublin schoolgirls.

Joan and I had subscriptions to comics or magazines—starting with *Tiger Tim's Weekly* and graduating later to *Girl*, and then the more serious *Children's Newspaper*—which were delivered on Fridays. We would hurry home from games for an R.T. (Reading Tea) and relaxation at the end of the week.

Loewenthal girls at Lennoxvale, c.1922
Photograph taken by Robert J. Welsh
Standing: Helen, Amélie and Peggy
Seated: Joan

I recall also a severe scolding from my eldest sister, Helen, when my friend Ethel Glendenning and I got a lift home from school with a friendly coalman. We sat happily on the back of the empty, dusty cart, hanging our legs over the back while the horse clip-clopped down the Malone Road. Helen said we were disgracing the school, wearing our Richmond Lodge blazers while behaving thus.

I left school in summer 1930. I had been made Head of the School during my final year. No prizes were given at Richmond Lodge, but on leaving each girl could choose a book which was bound in fine red leather and inscribed by the headmistress. I chose a volume of the complete works of Shakespeare.

Girl Guides

During the summer there was a two-week Girl Guide camping vacation under Miss McD's guidance which was a great education in itself. We learned to use our eyes and our imagination and to take responsibility. Oh, the excitement of preparing a kitbag and a sleeping bag made of two old blankets sewn together—no quilted, zipped-up present-day luxury! There was also a sack to be filled with hay and used as a mattress.

I have wonderful memories of sleeping under the stars, and of the deep peace of the night, broken only by an owl's screech or by bats flying overhead, and waking as the sun rose, one's top cover and pillow damp with dew, save for the spot where one's head had been lying. We awoke to dew on the grass and bracken sparkling in the early light and the smell of the damp earth drying in the morning sun.

It was only at the end of the first day, when at nightfall we got into our canvas bell tent and I was lying next to our patrol leader, that I was overcome by a great wave of homesickness. I poked her timidly and said: 'I feel sick'. A drowsy, cross voice replied: 'Put your head under the brailing and go to sleep'. Realising this was good advice, I went to sleep. The following days were so full, with the joy of sleeping, eating and cooking in the open, that I no longer wished to return home.

The Girl Guide camp at Glenarm, c.1923
Peggy front row far right

At the end of one camp holiday in Donegal the bus that was taking us and all our equipment to the train was late, and as we neared the station we saw the little engine puffing off. The driver sounded his horn and we all waved and shouted, and the train stopped. We then clambered out of the bus, ran across a field, dragging tents, pots and pans and baggage, and climbed onto the train for the journey home.

Oh, the joy of the first bath after two weeks of washing in the cold water of a stream or in a tin basin filled from a bucket of well water!

I remember, too, another year when, upon arrival, Miss McD asked me to climb up a grey stone wall that surrounded the estate on which we were to camp. She wished to know if it would be possible to bring all our equipment over the wall, as there was no nearby gate. I was then about twelve, already a Guide for a year and feeling quite senior, and I replied: 'Yes, it's fine. Tell the kids to come on.' Miss McD said nothing but gave me such a disapproving look that I still remember her reprimand. But it is thanks to her that I have such happy memories of days spent in the open air, and of the joy of being out in all weathers in the beauty of the Irish countryside.

A year or so later, at another camp, all the others having gone off on a hike, a friend and I were left alone in the camp to await the arrival of the fisherman with herrings for our lunch. Money was left with us to buy four dozen herrings and to have them cleaned. The fisherman came with his little donkey cart, the herrings were duly bought, and it was only as I was watching his silhouette on the brow of the hill that I remembered that I had not asked him to clean the fish, as I had been told to do. My pal and I set out to do the job, and it was nearly completed by the time the group returned. But it was a long, messy job, with no running water!

Growing Up

With the Bridels

In 1930 I was a teenager with my school days behind me. My mother was ill, having had a nervous breakdown some years earlier from which she never recovered (at this time very little was known about mental illness). My father wished to take her to Switzerland for treatment in a clinic at Nyon on Lake Geneva, and so we were driven there in our big old Sunbeam car by Alex, the chauffeur/gardener (who later married our cook Lucy, who stayed with us for many years). I was going for one year to Lausanne to stay with a Mme Bridel on the Avenue Nord d'Or and learn French.

Here I spent a happy time with four other girls, having French literature lessons with the old lady, a widow whose husband had been a pastor. They had four children: Mlle Marie, a schoolteacher at the lycée; Yvonne, who gave me piano lessons; Charles, an artist; and Gaston, a journalist. Yvonne and I played piano duets, which we got from a music library, and though I played very badly I did enjoy these lessons. I also went to a cookery course and did a little dressmaking.

Peggy in Lausanne, 1930, at the home of Mme Bridel

It was in Switzerland, when we all went to the mountains for the winter holiday, that I first learnt to ski. In the spring we also went on excursions, and I recall beautiful fields of white, strongly scented wild narcissi on the mountain slopes.

I slept in a room on the first floor with a little balcony. It had been the study of Pastor Bridel, and my bed was in the corner where his desk had stood previously. One summer night when the balcony door was ajar I woke up to find a strange young man in a beret but without shoes standing by my bed. He seemed as startled as I was when I turned on my bedside lamp. I grasped him firmly by his two wrists (rather in the way a drowning person grasps his would-be lifesaver) and said in my best French that if he did not disappear before I counted to ten I would shout for help. 'N'appelez pas—je m'en vais, me m'en vais' (do not scream, I am leaving, I am leaving) he said, smelling rather of drink. I let go of his wrists and he disappeared through the balcony door. I then went and woke up the old lady, saying: 'Il y a un homme dans ma chambre'. With her white pigtails and no teeth and in her nightgown, she came from the next room saying: 'Où est-il?' my having used the present tense in my agitation.

Then the two daughters, Yvonne and Marie, appeared and phoned their friend the policeman. He in his turn asked Marie if I had 'un amant dans la ville'. This shocked the old lady, who vouched for my behaviour. He then thought I had had a nightmare—'un cauchemar'—and I began to

Skiing in Austria in the 1930s

hum the latest tune from the film *The Congress Dances*, 'Ce n'est qu'un rêve, un joli rêve, c'est bien trop beau pour etre vrai' (it is but a dream, far too good to be true).

However, at this point footprints were found in my room and in the garden by the pillars that supported my balcony. The police then left, I shut the balcony door and we all went back to bed. Next day in the local press there was an article, 'Bizarre Apparition', written by Gaston Bridel, in which I was described as a 'jeune fille d'honorabilité parfaite'.

Charles also teased me by sending a note signed 'Cercle Rouge', as if it were from my 'intruder' (I still have this in my possession).

London, then back to Belfast

After a pleasant year with the Bridels I returned home to Lennoxvale to keep house for my father. I also took various courses at the Belfast College of Technology: English literature, chemistry and domestic science. Spare time was filled with tennis, youth hostelling and sailing with friends who had boats in various little harbours along the coast.

Then I decided to do a course in dietetics at the London School of Dietetics, which sounded interesting from its brochure. A week before I was due to begin, the school went bankrupt, so I joined a similar course at Battersea Polytechnic.

Peggy (left) and Joan on holiday in France, 1936

In London I got a bedsitter in Oakley Street in Chelsea. The course was interesting, and we visited several food production factories, including Lyons. I remember the conveyor belt on which twelve miles of jam rolls were made in twenty-four hours and girls were splashing on strawberry jam by the handful. This must have been approximately 1937. Later, when I became a factory inspector, I realised what changes had been made.

My year in London was uneventful and pleasant, with theatres and concerts. But I returned home, as my father was living on his own. I had hoped to find work in the Victoria Hospital but at that time there were no openings for dietitians in Belfast, so I went back to various occupations and voluntary work with the local Belfast Council of Social Services and the Arellian Nursery School, which was run by old girls of Richmond Lodge School (Arellian = R.L.'ian). This nursery school was the first one in Northern Ireland and was started in 1928 as the brainchild of two Arellians. It opened in a little dilapidated hall in a very poor area of the city, with six children, one paid worker and a volunteer staff of Arellians. This was a period of great unemployment, and poverty was extreme. Children were often sewn into their garments in winter, with an extra layer of brown paper for warmth.

The mothers paid two shillings and sixpence per week per child. They were known as 'shawlies', as they wore black woollen shawls instead of coats, which were more costly, and most of them were workers in the linen mills. Numbers grew so rapidly that larger premises were needed and local government became involved. A piece of open ground at the end of the street was made available, and a new open-air nursery school was built, which opened in 1931. This was later extended and is still running. The ground bordered the railway line, and I remember how one could always distract an unhappy toddler or anxious child by picking it up and going to look over the fence at the trains puffing past.

In 1941 the Belfast Council of Social Welfare, founded by my father, helped Queen's University, Belfast, to run a one-year trial course of Social Science, which developed into a full degree course; in 1942, having attended this short course and passed the Queen's University examination, I obtained a certificate of Social Science from Queen's.

War Work and Refugees

The Belfast Committee for Refugees from Germany and Austria

In 1937 my sister Helen came home to Belfast on a visit from London with details of the large number of refugees from Nazi Germany that were arriving in the UK and suggested that some help should be given by the people of Northern Ireland, so I arranged in our house a meeting with old girls from our school.

It was decided that we should form a committee under the umbrella of the Joint Christian Churches in Northern Ireland—Catholic, Protestant, Methodist, Quaker etc—and I became the secretary of the Belfast Committee for Refugees from Germany and Austria. The local Jewish community already had such a committee. They brought a lot of young people to a farm they had started near Millisle, County Down, hoping to train them for a future in Palestine, later to become Israel. Also they were able to bring a great number of refugees to the UK, as their guarantors were prepared to sign many guarantees, knowing that somehow someone would help once these unfortunate people arrived.

Our Committee did its best in getting people out on work permits, domestic permits etc, and children were taken in by private families and a few individual guarantees. This was in contrast to the Jewish Community Committee which, although they dealt exclusively with "true Jews" as opposed to all perceived as being under threat, such as non Jews with a Jewish spouse or grandparent, were aware of the situation in Germany and signed endless guarantees etc regardless, just in order to get people out. Unfortunately I do not think that any of us at that time had any idea of the horrors that were going on in Germany and Austria.

The work developed so fast that shortly our committee got a paid secretary who was herself a refugee with a seven-year-old son.

I was still very busy and had a car, so I often met these anxious and weary travellers as they got off the boat in the early morning in Belfast. Frequently I brought them home for breakfast and explained a little about their new life in Ireland, where they would live, something about their jobs and so on.

I remember the arrival of a Mrs Prince who came off the boat with two small children, and a canary in a birdcage. I also remember Dr Kurt Sachs, a psychiatrist from Vienna who was no longer so young and had great difficulty getting acclimatised to a new life. He came to our house often and relished a hot bath, as he did not have enough hot water in his digs. I quite unwittingly offended him one day when I met him in the street. He had not collected the small weekly allowance from the office and, as I had the envelope in my bag, I gave it to him then and there. He felt this street transaction to be terribly undignified and demeaning.

Then there was Joseph Frei, a young boy who had been offered a home by a kind but elderly spinster who spoke no German. The poor youngster, who spoke little English, was asked to varnish the sides of the staircase—a job invented just to give him something to do—and he mistakenly painted the carpet! He was rescued by the head of the Friends' (Quakers) Boarding School, where he settled happily. From there he qualified at Queen's University, Belfast, where he became a lecturer.

It is hard to imagine how these refugees from Hitler must have felt when war was declared on 3 September 1939, and the Home Office set up tribunals to try and sort out which aliens were genuine refugees, and whether there could possibly be Nazi spies among the many foreigners who had flooded into the UK in the previous few years.

We in Northern Ireland were comparatively lucky, as our Committee had an excellent relationship with the Northern Ireland government, Home Office and police. We were able to educate the locals in authority about Judaism, and what made a Jew, as all they knew of it until then was the small orthodox Belfast Jewish community. My close friendship with a local D.I. (Bill Moffatt) also facilitated communication with the police. It was often said that 'Peggy has the police in her pocket, ask her to get your permit'. We were able to send two representatives to sit on the tribunals that were set up under the chairmanship of a local King's Council (KC) to interview the refugees and sort them into three categories: A, those whose trustworthiness was doubtful, and who were taken into custody at once; B, those—and many of these unfortunate people fell into this category—who were unable to give definite information about their escape; and C, those who could prove their lives were in danger in Germany and who were therefore not suspect.

Peggy McNeill, an excellent Quaker member of the Committee, and I were allowed to sit, with the local police officer of the area concerned, as 'advisors' to Judge Begley, the chairman of the tribunals. All but one of these people were most sympathetic to the problem. Only the chairman was ignorant and ill-informed, in spite of the fact that the Committee had at the start given him all the details about the rise of the Nazi regime in Europe and the history of the persecution of Jews and liberals in the countries that had been overrun. This information was of little avail.

After several weeks he asked at one meeting: 'How is it that these children are here without their parents?' and we had to explain about children's transports arriving at Victoria Station, each child with a label on its coat with the name and address of a family in the United

Kingdom who had offered hospitality. (Ten thousand unaccompanied children were taken in by the United Kingdom before the war started.)

We had many grateful letters from these sad refugees, who appreciated both the assurance given by the presence of Peggy McNeill and myself at this 'inquisition', and the attitude of the Northern Ireland police.

It truly was a very difficult time, as no one knew whether or not Hitler's armies might invade our islands and the refugees once again fall into his hands. As it was, quite a number of the men under our care were shipped to internment camps on the Isle of Man. A few were even sent to Canada or Australia. We saw each of them off with a sleeping bag and a food parcel.

The only person placed in Category A (for immediate internment) was a young German boy teaching in the Berlitz School of Languages. An apologetic young policeman went to see him explaining the situation and asked 'Would Thursday week suit you?' He was picked up by a very sympathetic D.I. (District Inspector) who 'pub crawled' all the way to the prison. On his arrival at the gaol he found the cell prepared for him with flowers and fruit. That evening I received a phone call from Margaret Green, wife of the First Secretary of the Home Office, asking if Günther was Jewish. I said I thought not but why this question? She said she had made sausage rolls to send him in gaol and she feared that he might keep kosher.

The women who were classified as Category B after the interview we were able to keep in Northern Ireland, as the Home Office prepared a separate unit in Armagh Women's gaol for them, and Peggy McNeill volunteered to join them as a welfare worker. Ronald Green, an understanding and generous Quaker and Head of the Home Office at Stormont, came himself with deck chairs and bags of oranges to visit these unfortunate and distressed women. All were terrified that Hitler would invade and they would be caught.

One charming lady, who had escaped from Berlin with her seventeen-year-old son after her husband, a judge in Berlin, had been killed, remains in my memory. She wrote a most grateful letter after the tribunal interview which had frightened her terribly after her experience with the SS and the German police. She was shocked by the KC's ignorance of the situation when he asked if she had been forced to leave Germany.

The fact that Peggy McNeill and I were there to reassure her was much appreciated, but her son was taken as Category A to the police station, where later that day we were able to arrange his release because he was under 18 years old. I collected him and, to his mother's great delight, took him straight to a weekend outing in the Mourne Mountains Youth Hostel. Later Ernst joined the Pioneer Corps and was killed at the Battle of Arnhem.

During the time the women were interned in Armagh gaol the police constable who registered all the aliens in the police office in Belfast was promoted and transferred to another station, and the women wrote to thank him for his friendly courtesy and help, and to congratulate him on his advancement. The reply he sent with a covering letter to me was touching and was very gratefully received by the internees in Armagh. It was dated 7 August 1940:

> *With grateful heart I wish to thank you for the extreme kindness which prompted you and your friends to send me your letter of 27th which has now reached me. It has been my pleasure and privilege to have known you and I can assure you that any little I have done for you was a labour of love.*
>
> *May I send you my best wishes for the future and hearten rather than discourage you when I say that it is my earnest wish that the world will be a better place when you regain your liberty. In case it is not my lot to see you again, as my promotion has meant my moving from here, I send you these few lines, which have been an inspiration to me and I trust encourage you.*
>
> > *'Life is sweet because of the friends we have*
> > *made and the things which in common we*
> > *share.*
> > *We want to live on, not because of ourselves*
> > *but because of the people who care.*
> > *It's giving and doing for somebody else—*

on all that, life's splendour depends,
and the joys of this world
when you've summed it all up
are found in the keeping of Friends.'

Again thanking you. With kind regards I desire to remain your sincere friend, P.C. Hughes

One of the refugees who came to Belfast from Vienna in 1939 was a young lawyer Fritz Löwenkopf. His non-Jewish fiancée was due to follow him a few weeks later, but when she reached the Dutch coast on her escape journey she found to her horror that she had lost her cross-channel ticket, and the boat to England was about to leave. A Dutchman, who was a complete stranger, seeing her distress, bought her a ticket so that she could join her fiancé. After the war she tried to trace this generous stranger, but without success.

The couple married in Belfast. Our Committee arranged a honeymoon week for them and gave them a wedding gift. The wife earned their living as a dressmaker, as Fritz could not practise law in the United Kingdom. Their son was born in Belfast. In 1958, when I was in Vienna, I ran into Fritz (had changed his name to Lingardt) in the town, where he once again had a job and a home. Later his son married there and became a doctor.

Among those we managed to keep from internment in 1939 was Paul Ewald the famous crystallographer who had arrived to take up a lectureship at Queen's University. The

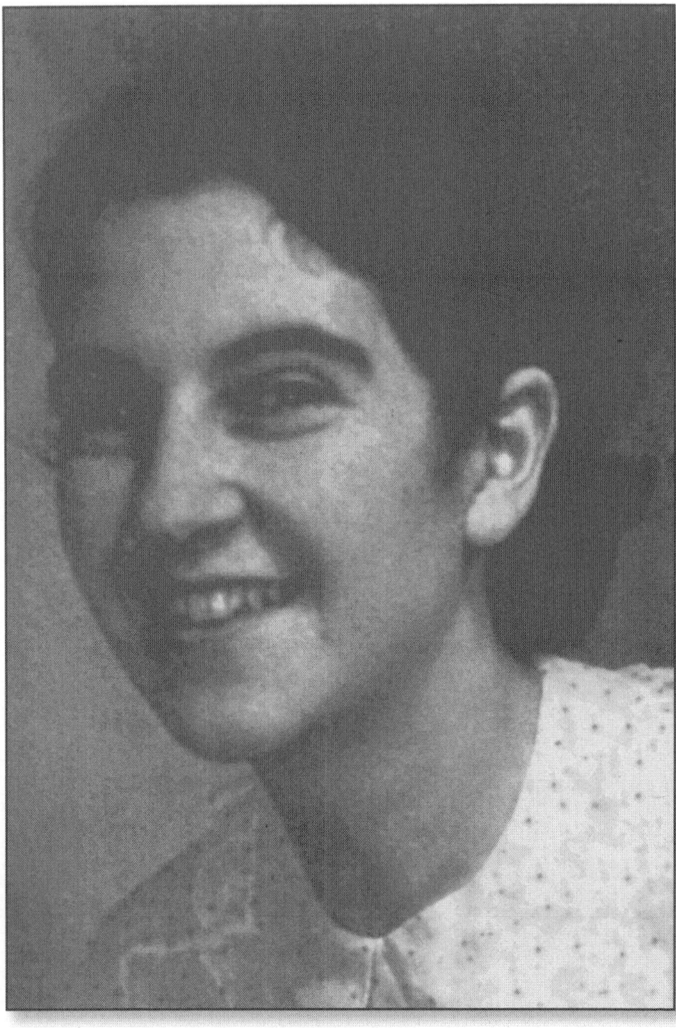

Peggy, c.1938
Portrait taken by Paul Ewald's son Arnold, when she was working in Belfast with refugees from Germany and Austria

vice chancellor was initially scared to take the risk of taking on this German scientist who had left Stuttgart only two years previously to be a research fellow in Cambridge.

It would have been during this time that I recall our home at Lennoxvale being used one day for what I was told was a secret meeting, and only my father, myself and Sarah the maid knew about it. Paul Ewald had become a close friend of the family. On that day he was meeting with Erwin Schroedinger the theoretical physicist and, I believe, Niels Bohr the nuclear physicist. I am not certain as to what they discussed, but I believe it was about keeping nuclear findings from the Germans.

1939: ARP (Air Raid Precautions)

During those first years of the war I worked for the ARP as a driver for Douglas Harrison, the Professor of Chemistry at Queen's University. He was the 'gas officer' for our district and he was responsible should there be a raid with poisonous gas; I had taken a course in First Aid. When there was an air raid warning and the sirens wailed, I would get my tin hat and gas mask and pick Douglas up and drive him to the ARP Centre in the city centre.

One night on my way to collect him the AA (anti-aircraft guns) were barking and shrapnel was raining down, and I noticed a biting smell in the air. When I saw Douglas I suggested that this smell might be gas and that we would look foolish if we were to arrive at the Centre without wearing our masks. Douglas took his litmus paper and waved it out of the car window, but it did not turn a different colour. Arriving at the Centre, which was the district police station, we learnt that a smoke screen had been laid over the shipyard for the first time, and it was this that had caught at the back of our throats. This raid caused severe damage to the town—some six hundred people were killed and many houses in the poorer parts of the town were destroyed. Even in our house in the outskirts of the city a window had been broken by the blast. I had to drive some of the ARP personnel to the bombed area, where fires raged and the streets were full of rubble.

Belfast suffered two bad air raids during the Blitz. One was Easter of 1940. I had spent the holiday in Dublin, which was only a hundred miles south and in a neutral country. (There was no rationing there, and no blackout. Very little was checked at the 'frontier', and many military put on mufti and visited Eire. The Germans also landed from submarines in the south. This led to the unusual situation of fraternization between men from both sides in the South of Ireland.)

On my way home, carrying six unrationed fresh eggs and butter and wearing three pairs of unrationed silk stockings on my legs (this was before nylon), I was standing in the corridor of the overcrowded train with the guard, who was trying to pull down the blackout curtains and having great difficulty pushing his way through the crowds, and I jokingly said: 'These lights would be a good guide to Jerry planes if they came tonight'.

When I got home and was enjoying one precious boiled egg, the sirens went. I ate my egg but had no time to take off my precious stockings. I fetched Professor Harrison and we were sent on to another station to help. I was given a cane chair on which to sit, a nail caught one leg and all three stockings on that leg came to grief. But it had been quite a bad raid and as that was my only casualty I couldn't complain.

About 1940 I spent three months in Scotland doing an emergency course in industrial welfare and personnel management. This was organised by the Ministry of Aviation under the minister, Stafford Cripps, because so many women were being drafted into the aircraft factories. The first month I attended Edinburgh University, and the second month we were attached to personnel departments in various factories. I thought I would be sent to Hoover but ended up in Jedburgh on the borders in a smaller viscose factory. I looked forward to the fresh air and beautiful countryside of Jedburgh as I remembered it from previous visits, but was taken aback by the smell of sulfuric acid which met me as I alighted the train! The final month was spent in Edinburgh, and then I had to return to Belfast to be with my father.

I soon had a job in Belfast as personnel officer in a branch factory of Short Brothers, who were making Lancaster bombers and Sunderland flying boats and employing some two thousand workers, four hundred of whom were girls. I was supposed to check welfare conditions, hiring and firing of the girls and canteen services, and to have contact with the unions and be a go-between generally for management and workers.

This type of work was new in Northern Ireland, and both sides of the industry were rather suspicious of me at first, as I was more or less forced upon both sides, but I soon made friends.

Billie Beatie, the convener of the AEU (Amalgamated Engineering Union) was a splendid chap who came to my office for long chats about many of the social problems of the day. He later made me an honorary member of the AEU. On the other hand, his opposite number in the electrical union was a far-out Communist who distrusted me completely.

Management was very suspicious of me at first but soon learnt that I could be of use in smoothing out difficulties and acting as an intermediary in certain disputes arising out of workers' personal problems. When I left a year later the director gave me a very nice letter of recommendation and the girls presented me with a gold watch.

The one expert personnel manager in Northern Ireland at this time was Mrs Gilmore, who was in the Factory Inspectorate at Stormont. She was very keen to improve all branches of social reform and felt strongly the need for a second woman in her department. The Ministry of Labour offered me the job of factory inspector and training in this field. I expected to do a course of several months but instead was sent to Glasgow for ten days to work with the Paisley Inspectorate and then returned to Belfast and was sent out, under the Factory Act, to inspect local factories and workshops.

It was a very interesting and often amusing experience. After having been shown through one small handkerchief factory in Victoria Street, and having made a long list of things that needed attention, I asked to speak to the manager. He was at a meeting, so I said I would wait. Then, to my embarrassment, out came George Thompson, one of my friends, who it transpired ran the factory with his brother; he was equally astonished. One did not inspect premises owned by people one knew! The improvements I recommended must have cost a considerable sum.

Randal Garrett was another friend in the Factory Inspectorate at Stormont. He later joined the Air Force. One day when Amélie took the boys to the beach at Tyrella he swooped them with his plane, terrifying them all!

I was a civil servant for two years, during which I learnt a great deal.

But when in 1945 the war was over, and Joan, whose husband was still in the army for another year, came home to take care of our father, I decided to try to get to Europe with one of the many relief units working there.

AJDC (American Joint Distribution Committee)—Going to Belsen

During my summer leave in 1945 I went to London and applied to several of the relief organisations: Quaker Overseas Service, Jewish Relief Union, British Red Cross and United Nations Relief and Rehabilitation Administration (UNRRA). UNRRA offered to send me to China, but this was a three-year contract, and I didn't want to be away for that long as my father would have been on his own. All the other organisations asked me to fill in forms and said they would advise me in one to six months. I was staying with my sister Helen, who also had an American visitor in the flat. When she heard of my desire to get to Europe she asked if I had been to the American Jewish Joint Distribution Committee in Piccadilly, of whom I had not heard before.

Next day I telephoned for an appointment with the director, Commander Harold Linder (who later served in the Kennedy administration) and I went the same day to see him. I explained what I had been doing during the war and described our work before the war for the refugees in Belfast and said also that I spoke French and a little German. He told me to come back after lunch, and on my return he said he had telephoned his headquarters in Paris and they wanted me. When I asked him when they wished me to start, his reply was 'Yesterday'. As I had to give the Northern Ireland Ministry of Labour one month's notice, it was five weeks later that I was back in London to be 'processed' to start work in the Paris office.

I had to get a uniform—topcoat, tunic (with AJDC insignia on the shoulder), skirt, slacks, underwear (even these were khaki!) and so on—from Moss Bros., and also various injections. This meant a lot of traveling around London, and once when I was in the office I asked for a small amount to cover overhead expenses. The office staff were quite upset that my salary had not yet been settled, and, although I protested, as I had intended to do a year's voluntary work, they insisted on giving me a per diem allowance (which was as much as I'd earned annually in the Factory Inspectorate), plus a very adequate salary (equivalent to that of an army lieutenant), which they paid directly into my bank.

In the office at this time I met a Canadian, David Wodlinger, who was transferring to AJDC from UNRRA, where he had worked ever since he got out of the Canadian Air Force. He was going to the British zone of Germany as the first director of the Joint. As I was a British subject, he thought it would be helpful if I were to go with him to the Displaced Person's camp at Bergen-Belsen in the British zone and said we would discuss this idea when we got to Paris headquarters.

He left by plane and I by train and boat, but I got there first, as his plane had engine trouble and had to return to London. The Paris office was large and busy, and I learned about the foundation of the organisation, in 1890, to help Russian Jewish refugees to escape to the USA. In about 1930 the organisation had nearly come to an end, but the Nazi regime had created new refugee problems and forced a rebirth. The AJDC had been enormously busy ever since.

The people in the office were all extremely friendly and I was amazed when taken to eat at the USA mess. Steak and two eggs for breakfast, and white bread—a meal such as I had not seen for the past five years, as the UK was still strictly rationed. (The AJDC had vast funds collected by the United Jewish Appeal in the USA.)

Bill Bein, one of the directors, was leaving for Poland and asked if I would join his team, but I had already agreed to go to Belsen with David. We were to leave in a few days, taking two Jeeps and one Dodge ambulance, as transport was scarce in the British zone. We had two Displaced Persons and David as drivers. Then I remembered that in my luggage I had a carton of cigarettes to be delivered to one Egon Fink, who was working for a sister organisation, Oeuvre de Secours Aux Enfants (OSE, a Children's Aid Society), running children's homes for French orphans rescued from concentration camps.

These homes were in the Paris suburbs, so I telephoned Egon. We arranged to meet in a bistro on the Champs Elysée. Having no wrapping paper, I wrapped the cigarettes in newspaper, and at the bistro I met Egon, who was smartly dressed in mufti, topcoat and gloves. He looked at the newspaper parcel with disgust, put the carton in his pocket and tossed the paper away.

We had a drink together and I explained that I was off to Belsen the next day with AJDC. He told me he got all the finance for the OSE homes from AJDC and that these homes now ran smoothly, therefore should I hear of a 'challenging job' in Germany with AJDC he would be interested to know of it. So we exchanged addresses, then I left him to join a friend. Egon was cross, as he had taken the day off to show me Paris.

The cigarettes had come from a friend of my sister Helen's who had met Egon in the winter of 1938–39 when, as a Viennese refugee to France, he ran a ski school above Grenoble in La Morte. The friend, Evelyn Fitch, who had kept in touch with Egon, had written to say that he should show the 'jeune Irlandaise' (young Irishwoman) around Paris.

A few days after meeting Egon I left the Paris European Headquarters of AJDC, heading for Belsen with my boss, David Wodlinger. We drove the large Dodge ambulance, and the two DP drivers followed in the

Jeeps. Our first stop was Frankfurt, at a large I.G. Farben building, which was the UNRRA headquarters and full of hurrying, busy personnel.

Here I met two directors of AJDC, Herbert Katzki, who had been head of the Paris office during the war, escaping to Lisbon just before the Germans entered the city, and Harry Biel, who came with us to Belsen for a short period. I always remember Harry sleeping in the storeroom in Belsen, which was full of jerrycans, spare parts and so on, with little heating. He slept in his uniform cap, as he had a very bald head and felt the cold.

In the UNRRA I was given additional uniform from an AJDC depot: a warm duffle coat, a quilted sleeping bag and a pair of excellent leather shoes, all of a first class quality not seen in the UK during the war or since, clothing coupons still being in use. We also picked up a second ambulance, which Harry drove. As we continued our journey towards Belsen I joined him, with David and the two boys following.

By nightfall we had arrived at Kassel, one of the most badly bombed towns in Germany, and, having lost contact with the three other vehicles, we looked for accommodation. We stopped at a large bunker which was an air-raid shelter, but Harry was told that this was only for coloured personnel. While he was making enquiries a black GI came and relieved himself against the wheel of our Jeep, shouting 'What's the time, mate?' On my replying that it was 9.30, he said 'My God, a woman!' and fled.

We continued through the rubble to the next seemingly habitable building, only to be directed to the ENSA (Entertainments National Service Association) office, where we were made welcome, though they had only a two-bedded room free. Harry refused my offer to share it and bunked down on two chairs in the office while I had a good night's sleep. His excuse to the clerk was that I was the director's (David's) fiancée. (Not true!)

In the early hours David arrived, very cross and tired, as he had been searching for us all over Kassel.

David, having previously worked for UNRRA, wished to visit one of their stores to see if he could obtain supplies for Belsen, but the only surplus stock available was a large quantity of ladies' bloomers. These were piled high in the ambulance, in which one of the DP drivers and I then proceeded to Belsen. Every time this young man braked suddenly I was engulfed in an avalanche of bloomers.

Egon, February 1947

Egon: Growing up in Vienna

Early Childhood

Egon was born in Vienna on 13 October 1906. His eighteen-year-old mother, Johanna, née Gefaell, divorced her husband Emil Fink when Egon was six months old. He was their only child. Both Egon's parents remarried. His father had three more sons, Ernst (born 1912), Leopold (known as Poldi, born 1913) and Robert (born 1916). Poldi died in 1988 and Ernst in 2002. Robert and his mother Zali disappeared in Hitler's Holocaust, deported in October and May 1942 to Minsk and killed at Maly Trostinec.

Egon was brought up by his grandparents, Bettina and Samuel Fink, whom he loved dearly. Samuel was a clock mender born in Sanok, Poland, and had worked for the railways, mending the station clocks. Thus he came to Vienna, where he stayed in a tiny flat in Sechshauserstrasse. Here Egon lived, sleeping in a little room behind the workshop, surrounded by ticking clocks and watches. On Friday nights his grandmother would fill a wooden tub in front of the fire with warm water for his weekly bath. After being rubbed dry on her knee, he was tucked in to bed and would whisper 'Grossmutter, Du weißt schon' (Grandma, you know …). She would give him a piece of chocolate. He did not dare to ask aloud for this 'Betthupferl' (Viennese expression for a bedtime treat), since if his grandfather overheard he would crossly say, 'The child is being spoilt'.

One day when he was in his third year he was sitting on the doorstep in a peppita smock. His fair curly hair came to his shoulders. His grandmother called him in to the flat and dressed him in his first pair of trousers, cutting off his curls, to his great dismay. Then he was sent to the nearby kindergarten, but, whereas all the other children were fetched to go home, no one came for him. In his anxiety he wet his trousers. Finding his own way home in the nearby street, he entered the flat saying: 'Granny, look how the rain has made me so wet!'

About this time his grandfather took him to Mariahilferstrasse (a large boulevard in Vienna) and held him up so he could see, over the heads of the crowds, an old man with a white beard in a fine horse carriage. It was Kaiser Franz Joseph, travelling from Schönbrunn to the Hofburg. Some years later, when the Kaiser died, all the schools were shut and Egon remarked that he wished the Kaisers would die more frequently so that they could have more holidays. But he enjoyed his school, the 'Evangelische Schule' (a major Protestant school) on the Karlsplatz. At home he learnt Hebrew from his grandfather.

When he was about seven years old he went with his friend Willi Stern to the Prater, Vienna's amusement park, where he stayed out much later than he was allowed to, returning home and creeping straight into his bed. When his worried granny opened his door he said from under his quilt: 'Are you looking for me? I'm fast alseep in bed.' He had many other adventures with Willi, and one day they decided to run away. Having supplied themselves with a pot of jam and a sausage from the store cupboard, they set off along the Wienzeile, a stream that flowed through the nearby suburbs. Along its banks they took off their shoes and socks and played all morning. When they had finished their provisions and it was getting late, they decided that leaving home was not such a good idea and, forgetting their footwear, ran home to be scolded by a very worried and cross granny.

At the top of the Sechshauserstrasse was a little church where many of the local children were choir boys and bell ringers. As these children ran past Egon's door to ring the church bells, they would shout to him "Komm Jud', komm läuten" (Come on Jew, come bell-ringing). He would join them in the bell ringing and so earn a few groschen.

When he was still very young he was sitting on the kerb in front of the doorway when a strange man came up to him and gave him a sweet, saying: 'Go into the grocery shop [a little grocery next door] and say your granny wants to borrow a gilder'. The shop lady gave Egon the money and the stranger took it from the little boy. Some weeks later the shopkeeper demanded a repayment from Frau Fink, who was very bewildered until Egon confessed and explained what he had done.

He tried very hard about this time to learn to whistle—without success. He also had a great dislike of eggs, which he frequently had for his supper. So his granny said that eating eggs helped one to whistle splendidly. There was no more trouble at suppertime, and ultimately he did learn to whistle—but he never enjoyed eggs!

Near the flat in Sechshauserstrasse there were stables for the horses that took the milk carts around Vienna. Here Egon and his small friends used to play. They caught mice in the hayloft and would harness the poor little animals to matchboxes and, making tracks in the sandy earthen floor, would have races.

On Sundays, dressed in his sailor suit and patent leather shoes, he went with his grandparents for a walk to Schönbrunn. Once when passing an open space he saw all his friends playing a football match, and one of the boys shouted to him: 'Come, Gondi, and help us win the game'. Before his granny could stop him he was in the middle of the scrum. Long trousers got torn and became shorts, patent shoes split, but their side won the game! At the Evangelische Schule he enjoyed his geography and history lessons and began to take an interest in politics and the growing social-democrat movement. When he attended political meetings his granny always told him 'Geh hinter dem Julius' (walk behind Julius), meaning that if there was a rally he would be sheltered behind Julius Deutsch, who was the Socialist State Secretary for Defence in the early twenties, a social democrat deputy to the National Council from 1920 to 1933, and the founder of the Schutzbund. Egon was an active Socialist and a member of the Schutzbund. In the February 1934 civil war in resistance to the rising fascist movement, he was injured during the failed defense of the Karl Marx Hof. It was this which ultimately made Egon decide that he had to leave Austria.

Leaving Home

His grandmother would worry when he went off on skiing trips with his friends, warning him 'Geh nicht auf dem Rand spatzieren' (don't go walking along the edge). Never having been in the mountains herself she thought the 'edge' would be a dangerous place! His grandmother died in 1922 when Egon was fifteen, and his grandfather remarried, but Egon could not get on with this lady and so when he was about fifteen years old he left home.

On one skiing trip Egon and his friends returned tired and hungry to the valley and went into a Gasthaus for a meal. Egon, having little money, ordered a Gulaschsaft (goulash gravy) and a hunk of bread. When the waiter brought the bill Egon realised he'd been charged for a plate of goulash, and he wouldn't leave till the waiter brought him a plate of meat, which had been omitted from the sauce.

Egon was sharing a room in Vienna with Hans Golding and could only go home when no swimming trunks were hanging out of the window, for the trunks were a sign that Hans had invited his girlfriend home.

While most of his free time in winter was spent in the mountains—he was a champion skier—summer weekends were spent canoeing on the Danube and camping on a nudist island with Willi Stern and other friends. Willi's mother would invite Egon for a meal and when she said 'oh do finish this up, it will only be thrown out, Egon', he was much too proud to accept, though he was ravenous. Later, at home and still hungry, he would regret his pride.

One summer when he was about seventeen he and Willi Stern set off on a Wandertour (rambling tour) through Germany and Switzerland, doing odd jobs to earn their keep, staying on farms and in Salvation Army hostels etc. One evening they were walking along a Swiss lakeside and they met a young man in white, with a tennis racquet in his hand, who asked them where they were going and what they were doing. He then offered them a night's lodgings in his nearby villa, where they were received by a fat, kind cook who gave them a good meal, then a bath and clean bed and took good care of them, as her own son was also off on a Wandertour of another country. Next morning when they went to say goodbye and thank the master of the house, he shook hands with each young man. On the road again Egon said 'Willi, he has given me a coin'. 'Me too,' replied Willi, and as they opened their clenched fists each lad saw he had been given a small gold coin.

In his early twenties Egon fell seriously ill with mastoiditis and was in hospital, where they thought he would not recover. A friend who was visiting him tried to cheer him up and promised that when he was better he would be given a fine new pair of ski trousers from the friend's father's factory. Egon did recover, and when he was discharged from hospital he went straight to his friend to collect his ski trousers, to be greeted with the exclamation: 'Oh, we didn't expect you to get better.' But he did get the ski pants. He remembered the hospital priest putting a cross on his chest when he was so ill and just having the strength to explain that he was sorry but he was Jewish. Although he recovered from this illness, he was deaf in one ear from that time onwards.

Egon had worked at various trades but then settled with his Uncle Max, who had a small Golddruckerei (gold printing business), printing names in gold on leather hatbands etc. At night he went to night school and at weekends he was off to ski in the mountains; he also got very involved in the then growing Socialist Party. His rather spoilt and pretty cousin Regi would visit from Czechoslovakia, and he would try and educate her, and make her work peeling the potatoes and helping with the meals etc. When she refused he locked her in his room till he came back from work for a meal. His meals at this time were often very frugal—stale buns from the next door bakery that were sold cheaply, and a kilo of blueberries with sugar.

Egon saw little of his parents. His mother remarried and after the war he traced her to the Argentine, where she had lived with three daughters, having managed to escape Vienna to Bolivia in 1939, but sadly she had died just after the war. His father also married again and had three sons, Ernst, Leopold (Poldi) and Robert, who was deported with his mother and did not survive. Ernst married and left for Palestine in 1935, where he had two married daughters and eight granchildren. Leopold married Renée, the daughter of a non-Jewish couple who had hidden him in France during the war, and settled in France; he had no children and died in 1988.

During the Socialist uprising in 1934 Egon was involved in the fighting around the Karl Marx Hof in Vienna (the first working men's housing project in Europe, built in 1921). Here he was wounded in the shoulder, but he was admitted to hospital as a 'skiing accident'. Otherwise he would have gone to prison. After this, and also because of growing anti-Semitism, he realized that he should leave Austria. He was able to get to Paris as a representative of a Socialist sports paper (probably the *Neue Freie Presse*). Arriving in Paris with very little money and no knowledge of French, at the station he followed the crowd to the Metro, and then to the ticket office, where he handed over his fortune—ten francs—and received a weekly Metro ticket and two francs change. Unable to say anything, he got onto the train and, recognizing a wide avenue as the Champs Elysées, he got off and wandered down it. Coming to a garage he was just able to make out a notice in the window stating that help was required to wash cars. This work needed no French and was Egon's first job in France. He met an Austrian friend who worked on night shift, so they shared a room, with the bed occupied Cox and Box style, both night and day.

One day when the head of the garage was away Egon drove a couple of cars to a different parking place to get at a car requiring washing, and when his boss returned and enquired who had moved the vehicles Egon said he had. Realizing that he had a driver, the boss arranged for Egon to deliver cars that had been left in the garage overnight. One morning Egon took a large car to a client who was a Deputy and, upon being questioned by this man, told him how he came to this job. The Deputy suggested that Egon might go with him as secretary to South America, where he was being sent on a mission, but Egon declined this invitation. However, it was then arranged that Egon should go to a trade school to learn French and bricklaying. At this school he discovered that all the students left for the mountains to ski at weekends. He at once sent to Vienna for his skis, and when the school saw how well he skied (he had been reserve for the Olympic team), they asked him to become a sports teacher for the school.

So for several winters he was a ski instructor, and in summer he supervised the swimming pool.

Later he got the opportunity of becoming a representative for sports articles and, as a traveling salesman, visited many parts of France. One day in Monte Carlo he met a friend and they decided to have a day off. They met two girls who suggested that they should all go to the Casino. Egon had no luck gambling and soon had lost all the money in his pocket. Undaunted, he went out and sold his car to a man he met in the street. Returning to the tables, he slowly started winning, and when he again had the amount he'd received for the car, he decided to go out and buy it back. But the man demanded a considerable increase in the price and Egon returned once again to the tables. His luck held and he finally bought back the car. But after that experience he never gambled or played cards again.

During the Spanish Civil War Egon was near the French–Spanish border when friends who knew his political outlook asked him to drive a vanload of guns over a small byroad across the frontier. He agreed to do this, but unexpectedly was stopped by a Customs official, who asked what the cases in the van contained. 'Guns, of course,' replied Egon. 'Don't be silly,' said the Customs man. This bantering continued for several minutes, till the official wearied and waved him through.

In 1938, when traveling with his sports articles, he came to a mountain village where an old lady had a little shop. Egon showed her sports socks in various colours and sizes and she ordered several dozen in each size and colour, not realizing what a huge quantity the socks came to. They hardly fitted into her small store. But after the war Egon passed by again, and the shop owner blessed him and said the socks kept her and her family alive when there was little to eat. She could always barter socks for food.

Egon and his friend decided that the valley where this village was located was a natural ski terrain, and they got permission from the Mayor of La Morte to build two chalets. Egon, with his half-brother Poldi, who had now joined him from Vienna, built a small chalet with a little bar and called it 'Slalom'. His friend, with wife and family, built a larger chalet and let some rooms, and for the winter of 1938–39 Egon ran 'L'école de ski Fink'. There was little heating in Slalom and he and his half-brother had to break the ice in their water jug in their bedroom before they could wash in the mornings. One of Egon's first pupils in his ski school was Evelyn Fitch, a friend of my sister Helen.

World War II

At the outbreak of World War II in September 1939 Egon joined the French ski troops, Chasseurs Alpins, and was well thought of by his captain, as he was such an excellent skier. But one day it came to light that he was born in 'Vienne, Autriche' and not in 'Vienne, Departement Isère', and as a 'foreigner' (enemy alien) he was unable to remain in the regular French Army and had to transfer to the French Foreign Legion for the duration. Here he and Poldi served in the Wagia, Sidi Bel Abess, Timbuctoo and other parts of the Sahara until the fall of France, when the Petain regime came to power.

During the period Egon was in North Africa he had many adventures. One day in a desert camp he heard the sound of planes over the sand dunes and knew that the Italian Air Force was coming to bomb either the water wells or the camel enclosure, which provided the food and drink for the troops. As he wanted to avoid being bombed, he climbed up a flagpole so that he could see in which direction the planes were flying. At that moment Captain Naugez passed by and shouted at Egon 'Légionnaire, what are you doing up that pole?' Egon replied: 'Mon Capitaine, I want to warn the troops where the enemy is heading for—they are flying towards the water wells,' whereupon the bugles blew a warning blast and the men scattered in the opposite

Egon in the Foreign Legion
at Bin-El-Hadjna, Algeria, February 1940

direction. Next morning at roll call Egon was ordered to step forward and received a medal for bravery. 'Warning the troops in face of enemy fire.'

A very young Moroccan Legionnaire was frequently being bullied by a large tough German, who called the boy 'a dirty Jew' and ill-treated him. Egon intervened and found that young Cohen had given a false date of birth to be able to enlist, and that he was under age for the army. This was brought to the attention of the captain, and the boy was able to return to his family in Morocco. Many years later, when he worked in Casablanca with AJDC, when the head of a village Jewish community came to the office to request supplies for his village, Egon asked him if he had served in the Foreign Legion during the war. The young man said 'Yes, briefly'. 'And a certain soldier Fink slept next to you and helped you to get out of the army as you were only sixteen?' asked Egon. The man nodded. 'Well, Mr Cohen, I am that chap Fink', said Egon, to the visitor's great surprise.

One of the other Legionnaires was Fred Freed, a musician and actor who arranged many entertainments for the men and by the men. After the war Fred Freed worked for many years with Maurice Chevalier, writing his songs and sketches. We visited the Freeds in Paris in 1947.

During his service in the Sahara Egon got malaria and during one attack was ordered by the doctor to stay in his bed in his tent. All men had a period of quiet and rest during the greatest heat of the day, and at this time a tough sergeant ordered Egon to get up and do a job. Egon told him he was in bed by order of the doctor, whereupon the sergeant shouted and swore and kicked him in the ribs and struck him with an iron bar which happened to be in the tent. Egon's only defense was a nearby crate of bottles, which he lifted and dropped on his adversary. Next day the sergeant was divested of his stripes and Egon was left with a permanent scar on his lip from a blow of the iron bar.

Water at this time was extremely scarce and wine was rationed. Egon drank the water supplied for washing and shaved with his wine ration.

On another occasion Egon was in charge of a reprimand exercise. The Legionnaire in charge had also to do any exercise he ordered as punishment. Among the group on this day was an exceptionally unpleasant bully-type fellow, so with full equipment on their backs and guns at the ready they were ordered to cross a patch of desert at the double, and when halted to fall flat and prepare to shoot. Egon arranged to give the order to halt when the much disliked bully was in front of a cactus, while the rest of the group fell on the hot desert sands.

One day Egon was crossing the courtyard of their camp when a young American, Captain Hamilton, stopped him. Egon saluted, and was addressed by Hamilton: 'Legionnaire, do you eat chocolate?' 'Oui, mon capitaine,' replied Egon, noticing that a piece of silver chocolate paper stuck out of his uniform pocket. 'In that case you shall be my secretary,' said Hamilton. 'Mon capitaine, I don't type,' replied Egon. 'Well, get someone who does to work for you,' ordered Hamilton, 'as I drink and need a sober, chocolate-eating secretary.' Thus Egon got one of the easiest jobs in the camp.

He also was in charge of the canteen stores, and to bring a little variety to the diet he started trading dried foodstuffs with an old Arab who was growing dates and melons etc.

in a nearby oasis. When the camp moved the old Arab was so grateful that he insisted on giving Egon his daughter! He was very distressed when Egon refused the present, and as the lorries moved off the poor girl ran after them as far as she could.

After the fall of France, when Petain came to power, Egon was opening mail addressed to Captain Hamilton when he read a letter from HQ requesting the captain to fill out a form stating whether he was (a) a Freemason or (b) a Jew. Egon told Hamilton that this letter he must reply to himself, but suggested that it was now time to get themselves out of the army and North Africa. Egon had also been working at the petrol depot, refueling aircraft, and when France fell the pilots had been told to take off from this air base, and they would be given instructions as to their destination when they were airborne. As Egon was refueling the planes he told the pilots he would give them enough petrol to reach Gibraltar, and so a few more men and planes were able to continue the fight against the Nazis.

Then Captain Hamilton and Egon forged travel documents for themselves recalling them to France, with a group of 'Métropolitain isolés' traveling to France under a very young French sergeant. After a very rough voyage they arrived at the port of Marseille, where Egon suggested to the sergeant that he might like a drink of good French wine in the nearby bistro, and if so Egon would hold his briefcase with company papers and keep an eye on the group. The sergeant disappeared into the bistro for a quick drink, and Egon had time to extract his and Captain Hamilton's military carnets. Then the group was marched off towards the military barracks, and while passing through the very crowded market area, Egon and Hamilton broke away and separated in the mixed crowds. Egon made his way back to his little chalet above Grenoble and never saw Captain Hamilton again.

Then he joined the French Underground, the Maquis, which was very active in this area. Shortly after his return to France, he received a letter from England, from a friend of Evelyn Fitch, one Joan Russell-Roberts, saying that during her last stay in Grenoble she had forgotten her umbrella and asking Egon to go and fetch it at a certain address. He thought how mad these English are, but one day when down in the town he decided to go to the given address and rang the bell. The door opened and when Egon asked for the lost umbrella the elderly man said: 'Come in, come in. What can I do for you? Can I give you tea, cigarettes or butter?' (all extremely scarce at this time). Egon realized this was another cell of the Maquis and the umbrella was just a password. Another friend of Egon's in the Maquis, François Holzhuber, worked in the 'Petit Brun' biscuit factory. Here bombs were made from pieces of piping filled with dynamite to use against the German soldiers now occupying Grenoble. Years later when visiting the Holzhubers in their Paris flat Egon and François were talking about how the dynamite was stored under the bed.

Isette, the wife, nearly fainted in horror at this thought, as she'd been quite unaware of what François had for safe keeping in their room.

One day when Egon was crossing the main square in the centre of Grenoble there was a 'Razzia' and from all sides the German soldiers moved in, cutting off all exits and driving the people towards one narrow opening leading out of the square. Here two young soldiers in 'Feldgrauer Uniform mit Hundekettenverschluss' ("field-grey uniform with dog chain buckle", describing the uniform of the german occupation forces) were checking identity documents. Behind them stood a couple of military lorries, and those whose papers were not in order were being loaded onto them to be driven off to prison or camps. Egon had no official documents, and as he saw no way of escape to left or right he marched up to the two young Germans and, as if he were a German officer out of uniform, shouted 'Platz!' The two boys sprang to attention and saluted him and he strode out of the square—and out of danger.

After this Egon realized that if he was to remain in Grenoble he must have some official papers. He was thought to be French and non-Jewish. He was called to the Préfecture, where the German authorities wanted to send him to Germany as an interpreter, but he claimed his knowledge of German was inadequate. Other jobs were suggested and he still managed to make excuses. Finally he was ordered to go as a physical trainer on a youth scheme and was given a travel permit. He was able to change the date on this paper several times and thus was able to carry on his work in the Maquis.

However this was finally no longer possible, so when the Nazis were again on his tracks he decided to try to escape to Switzerland. He set off leading a party of refugees on skis, over Mont Blanc, and with some difficulty they got safely across the border. Egon, as he left, was suffering from a bad attack of sciatica. However he got so warm climbing on his skis that by the time he reached the safety of Switzerland he had recovered and was never troubled with this ailment again. At first he was interned in a military refugee camp and then he got himself transferred to a more comfortable civilian camp in Mezovico in the Tessine. Here he was befriended by Selma Gessner, a Swiss social worker in the camp, and her husband Robi, a well-known graphic designer with works in the USA Metropolitan Museum of Art etc., and who later gave us several of his pictures.

Egon used to tell our daughter Michelle of the canal the internees had dug during the ten months they were in the camp and I had imagined this to be quite a waterway. However, many years later we were on holiday in this area and Egon decided to show us where he had been interned towards the end of the war. The famous canal was part of a drainage scheme and quite small—but there was still a plaque stating when and by whom it had been dug. Then out of a tiny level crossing railway station building came a large grey-haired Swiss railway official who recognized Egon and, greeting him warmly, said: 'It is very strange, all those years ago you boys used to be happy to come into the warmth of my little office for a glass of wine and a chat. Now you all return in big cars, with beautiful young wives and here I still remain, the railway guard at Mezovico.'

1945: Paris, and Peggy

At the end of the war, Egon found himself back in La Morte and the Grenoble area, wondering how to make a livelihood. He went down to Grenoble and, meeting some of his old friends in a café, discussed this with them. They said it was easy and gave him a watch to sell which had been smuggled over the Swiss border. From this profit he bought two more watches and gave them to a girlfriend to sell. By the end of the week he had a wad of notes in his pocket and realized that this was not the way he wanted to make a living. He also decided that, having been lucky enough to survive the Nazi holocaust, and hearing that his half-brother and stepmother had perished, he would like to do some Jewish refugee relief work for a year before settling down. He went to a French Jewish Social Welfare organisation, Casip–Cojasor, in Grenoble to enquire about jobs, and the man behind the desk was also called Fink. His grandparents had come from Sanok, as Egon's had done. No jobs were available but Egon was offered cash relief. Pulling out his wad of notes he explained that was not what he was looking for, but he left his address.

Some weeks later Cojasor offered him work, organizing and looking after children's homes in the Paris area, where orphaned French survivors of the concentration camps were being collected and cared for by the Jewish Children's

Aid Society, Oeuvre de Secours Aux Enfants (OSE). Thus Egon came to Paris and after starting one home successfully he moved to do the same work at Fontenay aux Roses. It was from here that Egon came to meet me on the Champs Elysées, to collect a carton of cigarettes which my sister Helen's friend Evelyn Fitch had given me to deliver to him when I came to Paris in 1945 to work for AJDC.

Egon invited me for a drink in the bistro and I told him I was leaving in two days for the British zone of Germany, to work for AJDC. He told me that all the money for the OSE children's homes was provided by the AJDC and that the homes he had organized were running smoothly, so that if I heard of a challenging job in Germany I should let him know. I took his address and said I must leave to meet a friend.

Peggy and Egon: Belsen, 1945–1948

Belsen

The concentration camp at Bergen Belsen, in which an estimated 70,000 people had died, was liberated by the British troops on 15 April 1945. Brigadier General Glynn Hughes, who had been Deputy Director of Medical

Oven from the Bergen Belsen Concentration Camp crematorium

Services of the British Army on the Rhine, did amazing work at the liberation of the camp, where typhus was raging amongst the 58,000 inmates. Many young medical students from London who, like the rest of the world, were shocked at the appalling situation, came out to help at this time. During the first days of liberation some 1,500 people died from typhus and starvation.

Jossel Rosensaft, a Polish scrap metal merchant who was among the survivors, described the day of liberation: 'Freedom dawned over Belsen with the arrival of the British troops.' With little strength left, Rosensaft was bedridden among the corpses and the dying.

On 17 April 1945 two hundred of the survivors who were strong enough to walk met in one of the huts (no. 86) and elected a Jewish Central Committee, chaired by Jossel, to help reunite separated families, assist in physical and spiritual rehabilitation and organize political programs.

By May the old camp had been burnt down to prevent the spread of typhus, and later a simple stone memorial was built at the entrance, with a notice which read:

> *This is the site of the infamous Belsen concentration camp liberated by the British on 15th April, 1945. 10,000 unburied dead were found here, 13,000 have since died. All of them victims of the New German Order and an example of Nazi Kultur.*

Sign put up by the liberating forces at the gates of the Bergen Belsen Concentration Camp

Gradually most of the non-Jewish displaced persons (DPs) had been repatriated, but the Jewish DPs had no wish to return to the countries where they had lost so many of their families and where they had been so brutally treated, so that eventually the only survivors in the camp were the Jewish DPs. News spread that Belsen was now a Jewish DP centre, and many Jewish survivors of other concentration camps arrived.

The Central Committee acted as a democratic mouthpiece of the camp inmates, formed of Hungarian, Polish, Czech, Lithuanian, Greek and other national groups, each with its own culture and traditions but now unified and determined to return to as normal a lifestyle as possible, even on a temporary basis. Schools were created, and a tent theatre in which plays in Yiddish were produced. Religious events were taken over by a surviving rabbi. There was also a children's home for orphans, from which in 1946 the children were transferred to Lünenberg and Blankenese near Hamburg. It was to the latter that Egon was to come as director.

As the DPs were deloused they were moved to what had been an SS Panzer training camp about four miles away. This was known officially as Camp 2, but to the survivors it was known as Belsen-Hohne. Here, over a large area, were concrete housing blocks and a fair-sized hospital, later named the Glynn Hughes Hospital.

It was on the edge of this complex that AJDC had living quarters in a house that had been used previously by SS officers. We shared it with the French and Polish military missions. These men were there to sort out their nationals and to help them return to their homes. After the military missions had finished their work and left the camp this house was used exclusively by AJDC, and a few Jewish DPs came to clean and cook for us.

David Wodlinger and I came to Belsen at the end of September 1945. I arrived in the ambulance with the DP driver. We found the villa allocated to AJDC, where

Peggy outside AJDC Mess in Belsen

my room was. David, having stopped at Arolsen to procure some necessary papers and permits, turned up only some two or three days later.

My room had a wooden floor and was sparsely furnished with a bed, a chair and a cupboard. A 'borrowed' lamp, rug and heater were later added through the kindness of a Canadian Air Force officer, David Smith, popularly known as Smithy (Michael Gelber, David Wodlinger and David Smith were all in the Canadian Air force. Gelber and Wodlinger came from large Jewish Canadian families, and David Smith was not Jewish). Some months later Smithy hurriedly reclaimed these luxuries, having discovered that he could not be demobbed without returning them.

It was also Smithy who collected me from the station in a car after my first home leave, and who, after wining and dining me very well, took me to the Canadian Air Force women's quarters, where he had arranged for me to spend the night. Unfortunately, I had rashly mixed champagne and cherry brandy, with dire results. I badly needed a walk in the fresh air, and while going round the block we were stopped by the military police. I remember hearing the MP's: 'Sorry sir, one of ours'. At this time military personnel were not allowed to fraternize with German nationals. Next day Smithy drove me back to Belsen.

The water in the bathroom in our Mess was heated by a wood-burning stove, and the wood supply was severely limited. In the centre of the camp there was an SS officers' bath house where we frequently went after work to enjoy an unlimited supply of hot water and to soak in a bathtub filled to the brim, a wonderful relaxation.

The day after my arrival I went in to the camp to the offices allocated to us. At first there was nobody there to tell me what to do, and I felt that I could have been of more use back in Belfast, but then I found several boxes of unopened letters, and when I started to open these and read them I found that they came from all parts of the world and were search enquiries for missing relatives and friends—husbands looking for wives, parents looking for lost children and so on.

So I set up the first search office in the camp, for which I was given a room in block GB2. It was heated by an old iron stove burning mostly green wood and smoking very badly. Someone produced a liberated typewriter and an empty box for a card index, and two young boys who had survived internment came to work for me. They got uniforms with an AJDC flash and some extra rations, and each day I gave them a list of names of people for whom I was searching. They went round the camp with a loudspeaker in a Jeep and posted lists of missing people on notice boards around the blocks.

They also checked with the Central Committee, who had made a list of people who had survived at the liberation. One of the youths, Laszlo Kramer—a fourteen-year-old—became a devoted slave, and our efforts developed

Peggy at work in the Belsen tracing office

rapidly and later linked up with the International Tracing Service. It was wonderful when we were successful, linking separated families, husbands and wives. But we also met with problems and disappointments. Sometimes a woman who had believed her husband to be dead had remarried. On such occasions the rabbi would advise the woman to divorce both men and then choose one. Or occasionally we thought we had found a child for a mother, only to discover that, although the name was correct, just one day's difference in the birth date meant that it was not in fact the missing child.

I received a tracing enquiry from an American director of the organization who was looking for his niece and had sent an affidavit for her entry into the USA. Olga Steiner was on the original list of survivors that had been made by the Central Committee, but the boys searched for several weeks without finding further trace of her.

There was at this time no control of the movements of DPs, nor any notification of deaths or accidents. I had almost given up hope of finding Olga when, one weekend, I was taken out to the officers' club in a nearby village by a young captain of the British army who offered to buy me a drink at the bar. I asked for a gin and tonic, and I heard him say 'Two gins and tonics please, Olga'. 'Olga who?' I asked. The girl said her name was Steiner. I told her to come see me in my office the next day, as I had an affidavit from her uncle in America.

At this time there was no emigration to the United States from the British zone of Germany, as the Americans wished to clear the US zone first, so would-be emigrants had to swear that they had been liberated in the US zone. When Olga came to see me she asked what she should do, as she did not wish to start a new life with a lie. Thinking it over, I told her, 'Olga, you must make up your own mind, but I think if I were in your place I would go south to a US centre and swear that I had been liberated there. You are not taking someone else's place, as you have your own affidavit, and there is no guarantee when the British zone will grant US emigration. Also there is very little chance of work or study as long as you are a DP in this area.'

A week later Olga was in the American zone. A few weeks after that she was processed and sent to New York, where she started to work in a hat shop. A few months later she was married, and when I visited New York early in 1947 she made me the hat in which I was later married. When my daughter Michelle was born in 1950, Olga knitted her a pretty pink dress. Sadly I lost contact with her after that.

The work grew and became very satisfying. By contacting families overseas many DPs were able to emigrate and at last start a new life after their awful experiences. Laszlo Kramer, my office helper, came one day and said to me: 'Peggy, I want to return home to Romania and see if I can find my relatives'. I gave him my home address in Belfast and asked him to let me know how he got along.

Some weeks later my father forwarded a card from Laszlo in which he stated that he had managed to reach Romania, which was now in Communist hands, but didn't think he would ever be able to get out again. He said he had been foolish to leave Belsen and the British zone. His parents were lucky, with no more worries about the future, as they had both been gassed by the Nazis. Then I heard no more of Laszlo, who was at that time about fifteen.

Some twenty years later I met Laszlo again. We were settled in Vienna, still working for AJDC, we were dealing with escapees through the Iron Curtain from Communist countries: Hungarians after the 1957 occupation by the USSR, Czechs after the fall of Dubcek, Poles, and then a wave of Romanians, all escaping through Vienna. One day I had a telephone call from Lotte Levenson, an HIAS (Hebrew Immigrant Aid Society) worker in Vienna who processed all refugees wishing to emigrate to countries other than Israel. She had worked with us in Belsen in 1946. She said she had a Romanian in her office who knew me. He had told her he had worked for AJDC in Belsen, and when she asked him if he remembered her, he replied that he could only remember a Mrs Montgomery of the British Red Cross and Peggy Loewenthal from the Joint. Lotte explained that I was now married and living in Vienna, and Laszlo came to our house. He told us a woeful tale of his return to Romania, and being in prison after having been liberated by the West. Once released, he had trained as a photographer. In the fifties he applied for an exit permit to go to Israel, but he had been refused and, having dared to try to leave the country, he was back in prison.

When at last he was released from prison, he no longer had a work permit and had to eke out a livelihood as best he could. Finally he got his permit renewed, and as he was a good photographer he did quite well, working for TV and earning enough at last to go on a vacation to the Black Sea. There he met a French girl whom he liked very much, and she said that on her return to Paris she would send him a French visa. Once again, in great fear, he applied for permission to leave the country and this time he was successful, but emigrants were not allowed to take any possessions with them.

Laszlo had made friends with some German TV men, and they agreed to take out some of his equipment. Also he knew a girl on the Russian airway Aeroflot who agreed to take some of his personal papers. This included a small snapshot of me in Belsen in 1945 that had been taken by Laszlo with a liberated camera. Laszlo took photographs of Michelle, Egon and myself at our house in Vienna. Egon said to him that he could imagine what a difficult existence he must have had, and Laszlo snapped a reply that it was impossible to realize what life had been like in a Communist country.

With difficulty I persuaded him to accept some money to help him start in Paris, saying that when he was on his feet he could repay me. He left a few days later for Paris, but we never heard from him again. I often wonder what happened to Laszlo, whether he was a Russian spy or whether he regretted his emigration to France. It was like an unfinished symphony.

Our life in Belsen was filled with events, some comic and some tragic, but the work was always fascinating and challenging.

The Warburg family, who were at that time in New York, had given AJDC the use of two large houses at Blankenese on the outskirts of Hamburg, and here David Wodlinger set up a children's home for the orphans liberated from Belsen. He chose four young women to run the home—Belgian, Dutch, French and American—all girls in their early twenties, but the children who had survived concentration camp were not going to pay attention to four young women. Windows got broken, nails were put in the water pipes to see if water really flowed through and attempts were made to flush tin boxes down the toilet. There were perpetual SOS telephone calls from Blankenese to Belsen.

After one such telephone call David said in despair, 'Peggy, what can be done to help the children's home?' I remembered my brief encounter in Paris with Egon Fink, who was then organising children's homes for OSE and had said that he wanted a job with AJDC in Germany. I took his address out of my uniform pocket and gave it to David, who wrote to HQ in Paris and asked them to check whether Egon was still available and whether he would come to Blankenese. So, after getting military clearance and approval at AJDC, Egon came as a Joint employee to the British zone early in 1946 and took over the running of Blankenese Kinderheim.

Egon arrived in the Belsen office with almost no luggage. He had been promised equipment but had practically only the uniform he arrived in. I had received various parcels of clothing from England for the DPs, including parcels from Evelyn Fitch (whom Egon had known well in 1938–39 when he taught her skiing in La Morte), so I was able to give him some pullovers, shirts and so on from the parcels she had sent me. Thus Egon found himself dressed in cast-offs from the husband of his ex-girlfriend Evelyn. He then moved to Hamburg and took over the running of the Blankenese Kinderheim with, I think, some 120 children.

When he got to Blankenese he found that each of the children—seven to fourteen-year-olds—was getting a kilo tin of meat per day. Even for starving children this was excessive, but when he took them off the ration the children went on strike, calling Egon a 'Kapo', which was worse than the SS. (Kapos were prisoners in the camps who voluntarily accepted authority over fellow prisoners and acted as members of staff, and were known as selfish, brutal, greedy and authority mad.) It turned out that they had been trading the tins for high prices on the flourishing black market in Hamburg. Egon finally allowed them to receive their rations as before, but he opened each tin so that they were no longer of any value on the black market.

Children and staff
of the Blankenese children's home
Egon front row centre

Egon organized sports activities and schooling and so on, and he played football and games with the boys. When he was told once by an older child that little Moische had climbed up the trellises on the house wall to the first floor he replied: 'I didn't tell him to climb up, so he had better find his own way down'. Soon the home was running smoothly.

One evening when he was on his own he was feeling very bored, so he picked up the telephone and asked the operator to put him through to Hamburg. When the exchange answered he asked them to get him Stuttgart and so on through half of Europe until he again got to Hamburg. When he finally asked for the children's home number, which gave the engaged peep-peep he must have held up the whole network!

We met frequently, either in Belsen or on short weekend leaves in Hamburg. Once I picked him up to go for a meal in the officers' club, where there was a football pitch sized parking lot with two small Volkswagen beetles in the centre. 'Park between them,' said Egon, and I, driving a large Dodge ambulance, reversed directly in to the back of one of them. When we looked we saw that it was the colonel's car, so we drove off and had a meal elsewhere.

After some months the children from Blankenese got to Israel with the services of the Jewish Agency over the 'Grüne Grenze'; the first transport that left Belsen was known as 'the Grand National'. The home was shut and

Egon came to work in the Belsen office, to take over the transport with its cars, trucks and some fifteen or twenty DP drivers. Later he was in charge of supplies and finally was helping with emigration.

Children in train leaving the Belsen DP camp for Palestine

We were all very busy, but every evening, after our meal (our rations were adequate, but there were very few vegetables or fresh fruit, so we all had vitamin tablets with our supper), we discussed the day's problems—emigration, case histories, tracing missing people, medical problems, contact with military personnel from the British Army of

The AJDC Mess

Back: John Fink (left) and David Wodlinger. Middle: Peggy on far right, next to Hilde Jacobstahl. Front: Lottie Levensohn second from left, Dr Fritz Spanier far right

Egon and Peggy with David and UNRRA boys

Back row from left: Egon, Peggy, David Wodlinger

Men in caps are UNRRA personel

the Rhine (BAOR) and other teams such as the Quakers, the English Jewish Relief, the Red Cross, and so on working alongside, and the Belsen Central Committee.

Many weddings took place in Belsen as lonely people made new contacts. Emigration and the possibility of starting a new life and joining broken families were the primary aims of the camp inmates, but Palestine still had a strict quota system, and England demanded work permits or guarantees of maintenance. It was not easy to get out of Germany, so there were attempts to get over the 'Grüne Grenze', i.e. to move illegally over the borders.

Wedding of John Fink, who had been liberated at Bergen-Belsen, and Alice Redlich, Belsen DP camp, 1946
Peggy and Egon 4th and 5th from left

The Exodus story was one such case. A shipload of survivors of the concentration camps tried to reach Palestine but was caught offshore and returned to Germany, causing great protests in the press.

Egon and I were on leave at this time in Paris, and on visiting our HQ office were asked by one of the directors (Herb Katzki, a very charming man), 'What are you doing here?' Egon replied, 'We are on leave'. 'Oh no,' replied Herb. 'Get back to Belsen at once and take care of people off the Exodus.' I went back to the hotel to pack while Egon went off to see what he could do with our holiday cash. (At that time there was strict money control at the frontiers.) He came back very happy but a little guilty, having acquired a gold Omega watch, which was a childhood dream (his grandfather had been a watchmender, and this was the best watch ever made).

The poor people from the boat were brought to a nearby camp, Pappendorf, and finally to Belsen. Some of the DPs there had already managed to get a number of Palestine entry permits, and they were generously passed on to the people from this boat.

One day David Wodlinger received a letter from a couple in America, who said that a young boy had written to them from a village not far from Belsen, stating that he was a relative and asking for help. They thought he could possibly be the son of a Polish cousin with whom they had lost contact. David went to the address and came back with a fourteen-year-old boy, also called David (Gross), who told the following tale—

> He had lived with his parents in Poland, not far from the German border. When the invasion started and there were bombing raids, the family escaped to the nearby fields, but his father and mother had both been killed by one of the bombs and he was left wounded. The advancing German troops found him. They tended his wounds and then, not knowing he was Jewish, took him along as a mascot. He almost forgot his Jewish background until one day he was with a group of SS troops in a beer cellar and he heard them boasting about a church filled with Jewish refugees that they had set alight. One of the SS officers had given David a ring containing poison, something the German troops had in case they were captured. He put this poison into some of the beer glasses.
>
> Later, when the allied armies were advancing, the soldiers left David in the care of a German farming couple. After the armistice he remembered vaguely that his mother had a sister who had emigrated to the USA. He could remember the name and something of the address, which was in Chicago. He wrote a letter, which finally reached the relatives.

I remember clearly the arrival of the child in our Mess. He was about fourteen. He looked like a little Nazi in high leather boots, and when he was introduced he clicked his heels and bowed. He was very arrogant. He stayed with us for quite a while. On Saturdays we had a free day, and one Friday David was with us on the river bank. I was sitting by a deep pool where all my friends were swimming. 'Aren't you coming in?' they shouted to David. He hesitated, and they called again, then he leapt in and I noticed that he struggled, sank, came to the surface and splashed around, and sank again. When he came to the surface again I caught him by the hair and then by an arm and hauled him onto the shore. I asked him, 'Can't you swim?' He shook his head. He couldn't, but he would not admit to being unable to do what the rest of the crowd could do. Later he was put on a children's transport that got to Palestine, and it was said that he became a freedom fighter in the Stern gang—the natural ending, after his early training.

I recall also a young German girl, non-Jewish, who was working for the military government in the telephone exchange. In the evenings, when the lines were not busy, she used to ask me if I would like to speak to my sister in London, and she would connect me with Amélie. This happened quite often with success, until one night as I was waiting to be connected a British voice—the major—advised me that it was against military government regulations for civilians to use the phones. As I was worried that Amélie might have been advised that I was trying to call her, I asked the major to inform her that I was quite well and only wished to say hello. This he did, but my telephone conversations with the family ended.

In spring 1947 the orphan children from Blankenese were transferred by the Jewish agency to Palestine. The code name for this journey was the Grand National (as there were so many hurdles to overcome on this perilous journey), and a small bronze brooch was made to commemorate the event. I had one of these brooches until recently, but have donated it to the Belsen Memorial Museum. On it are praying hands towards a rising sun and the words 'Grand National, Belsen Palestine 1947'.

Egon, Peggy and a member of the Jewish Agency at the station supervising departure of emigrants

Thus the children's home was finally emptied and Egon came to work with us in Belsen. At first he took charge of transport and supplies. We had quite a large group of DP drivers, and there were several large trucks and the old Dodge ambulance. Among the drivers I remember a Polish man, Willi Langer; a small, fiery Hungarian called Griescha; and Maurice Kiefer, who warned Egon that he must treat Peggy properly and well. Then there was Platzner, a large, tough chap who, many years later, came some hundred miles to Chicago to meet Egon, when he was on a fund-raising trip. When Egon enquired how he was getting on in the United States, he replied, 'Very well, I am now a president.' 'What are you president of?' Egon asked. He replied, 'Oh, just a small steel corporation.'

At the end of 1946 a German boy called Harry Kopf had taken over the Search Bureau so that I could move into work with the problem of emigration, the possibilities for which were still very limited. Emigration to the USA from the British zone was not possible yet; the Americans were still trying to clear the American zone first. Some South American countries were accepting applications, and Sweden took quite a number of people on special permits. Canada also accepted various categories of people; I shall never forget the day we received news that we could send two hundred tailors to Canada.

On one occasion I accompanied a transport of people as far as Copenhagen, where representatives from the Swedish Jewish Welfare came to take over the transport. These occasions were very emotional—parting from friends in Belsen who had shared so much hardship, and the thought of the chance to start a normal existence once again, not to mention the fear of a strange country and a strange language.

In 1946 a DP doctor who had worked for a year in the Glynn Hughes Hospital doing appendicectomies and other such things had been questioned about his medical training. It was discovered that he had never had any. He was transferred to work with the transport team, and in no time he was mending all the cars, trucks etc. Then he heard of the chance to get to Canada as a tailor. He found someone to teach him the trade, and in a couple of weeks presented himself to the Canadian immigration authority, who passed him, and he left happily to begin a new life there.

Ruthie Reichman was a young nurse who had herself been liberated and worked in the hospital. She helped several people who were unable to get transit visas for France and other such necessary documents. She loaded up several families in a synagogue wagon (a truck used as a mobile synagogue) and smuggled them over the French border so that they could continue their efforts to reach the countries of their choice.

My year's contract with AJDC came to an end in the autumn of 1946, and I was due to return to Belfast. At this point David suddenly proposed to me. I was very surprised and touched. I had no idea of his feelings, which he really had not shown. But by this time I had become very attached to Egon. On a short leave that we had spent together in Amsterdam, Egon and I had agreed that, if possible, I would arrange to have a winter holiday with him away from the stresses and strains of community life with AJDC, and we planned to spend two weeks on a skiing holiday in La Morte above Grenoble in January 1947.

Peggy and Egon at dinner in the staff mess

I had a tremendous send-off from Belsen. Moritz Keifer, one of our drivers, prepared a very ancient Porsche, decorating it internally with little bunches of flowers stuck in the corners. He drove me to Bad Oeynhausen in this splendid vehicle to catch my train, and so I returned to my home and my elderly father, and once again I got a very warm welcome.

At home in Belfast I was asked to give a talk at the Rotary Club. This is its transcript:

> 'There are two types of people in the world now: those who have been in a concentration camp and those who have not.' This remark was made to me by a Rumanian girl cellist who had been forced to play classical music in an orchestra outside the gas chamber in one of the Nazi extermination camps, to deaden the cries. From the experience I have gained during this past year, when I was working with displaced persons present in Belsen, I found this tragic statement only too true.
>
> Belsen—that word will remind you once again of the sickening horrors that were brought to light when the Nazi concentration camp not far from Hannover was liberated by the British army in April 1945.
>
> Very little now remains of this old camp, which was burnt down by the troops to prevent the spread of typhus, which was rampant. All that can be seen on this bleak clearing in the forest, surrounded by high barbed wire fencing, are the mass graves, at each a small square board stating 'Grave number 1 – 5,000 unknown dead', 'Grave number 2 – ...' and so on. A grim but now rusted and broken down incinerator stands in one corner. In the centre a small stone memorial has been raised to the 23,000 victims of Nazi persecution who perished in Belsen. It was unveiled last April at a ceremony commemorating the first

year of liberation. Some 7,000 persons attended this moving and impressive service; many of them had themselves been liberated here.

Standing on this ground, I always had a feeling of oppression and unutterable desolation. The skies appeared leaden and heavy overhead, and yet wildflowers, grass and heather, were once again growing over this wasteland. At the gateway in the surrounding barbed wire fence stands the notice written in English and German which reminds all those who visit this site of the atrocity: '10,000 unburied dead were found by the British army on their arrival, 13,000 died in the first month as a result of inflictions and illness during the Nazi period of internment. All were victims of the so-called new German order and Nazi Kultur'.

A short distance from the original camp is Belsen-Hohne Displaced Persons Camp, situated in what was previously a German military tank training centre. It consists of blocks of concrete barracks stretching for several miles, the nearest village being some kilometres distant. When I arrived in November of last year there were well over 10,000 displaced persons living in the camp. They could be divided into two groups: first, the Polish and Hungarian displaced persons, who had mostly come to Germany as forced labourers; second, the Jewish survivors of the concentration camps, who were of many nationalities—Hungarians, Czechs, Poles, Rumanians, Austrians and some Dutch and Germans. It was the second group with which my work was connected. The main difference that struck one when comparing these two groups of people was that with the Polish displaced persons there were frequently family units—father, mother and children together—whereas the other group was composed mainly of single individuals, often sole survivors of a large European connection. Early this summer the Polish Displaced Persons were repatriated from Belsen. Most of the Jewish DPs did not wish to return to their place of birth, where they were sole survivors of large families.

On my arrival I found that our team, which was working in cooperation with the other relief organisations and the British Military Government then in charge of the camp, was very understaffed and overwhelmed with work. Many of the letters arriving at our office were enquiries for missing persons, and it was decided that a special department should be set up to deal with this correspondence. So my work in the Search Office began. We dealt with enquiries from all parts of the world, and we searched in all parts of the globe for connections of the survivors in Belsen.

We worked in close contact with all other relief services and especially with the UNRRA Tracing Bureau and the Control Commission for German's

Central Search Office. Unfortunately, owing to the continuous and heavy pressure of work, we did not have an opportunity to compile statistics, but we were able to locate very many missing people, though sometimes we had to reply that the person sought had not survived.

Records of deaths at Belsen shortly after it was liberated were not available owing to the terrible conditions then prevailing, when so many thousands died and when medical and nursing staff were overwhelmed by the situation in which they found themselves. But the Jewish Central Committee which had been formed after the liberation had a list of Jewish survivors. When I arrived Jossel Rosensaft was the chairman of this committee.

A young Dutch girl working with the Red Cross told me how she was left alone in charge of an inadequately equipped block with some two hundred seriously ill patients. There were up to twenty deaths a night in this block. There were, of course, no lists of those who had died in the camp before liberation.

It was not always easy to ascertain if a person who was being sought was living at present in the camp, as there was continuous coming and going among the population, even though for a Displaced Person travelling was not easy. Naturally the DPs are not now under lock and key, though sentries at the gate check the identity of those who pass in and out of the camp.

In spite of these difficulties, we were fairly successful in our work of uniting scattered families. I remember a young girl who came one morning to our office in tears, with a letter in her hand. It was the first news she had had from her aunt in South America, and this contact had been made through our office. Plans for her emigration to Brazil were already under way, and she was overjoyed, as previously she had thought she had no relatives alive in the world and she had almost given up hope for the future.

One is often asked, 'But why don't these people return to their own countries?' After hearing some of their stories it is not often difficult to realise why this is not possible. Take, for example, a woman doctor now in Belsen, where she was liberated after years of concentration camp existence. Her father, mother, brother and sister, her husband and her little boy of four were all gassed and burnt in Auschwitz camp in Poland. It is not to be expected that this woman should return to a country full only of the memories of the horrors she had suffered there. There were thousands of cases such as hers.

Therefore emigration—emigration out of Europe—is what these people in Belsen are now waiting for. Little has as yet been possible in this way. Shortly after liberation Sweden generously opened her doors to many thousands who were strong enough to make the journey; now some very close relatives of those who are already there are able to obtain visas and join them. England also permits entry to certain categories; so a few more get a chance to lead a normal life again. We were also able to help a few people, who had entry permits to some of the South American countries, to acquire French transit visas, and thus leave the camp. A careful check is made by the authorities before permission to leave Germany is granted. As yet there is no emigration open to the United States from the British zone in Germany, except for non quota preference cases, which are very few, though many DPs originating on the American side have left from the USA zone. This is very hard indeed for very many people to accept.

Rosa, the cook in our mess, is an example. She is a dear person, kindly, thoughtful and patient. She said to me one day: 'You know, my children would be ten and twelve this year if they were alive.' She also had lost her entire family in Auschwitz. On her arm she had her camp number tatooed, like all survivors of Auschwitz. For in Auschwitz they ceased to be human individuals and became mere cogs in the Nazi machine. Rosa has received an affidavit from her sister in the States, who is prepared to house and keep her and is desperately anxious to do all she can to help, but there is still no news as to when Rosa and many others in the same position will be able to leave Belsen. She said to me: 'I must write cheerful letters to my sister because she would be so unhappy if she thought I was depressed.'

It is this cloud of despair for the future that casts such heavy shadows over the lives of those still in this camp, more than one and a half years after liberation. The longer such people are forced to remain in this depressing and demoralising atmosphere, the harder it will be for them to be assimilated into any normal society again, for it is impossible to organise any large-scale rehabilitiation programme in these surroundings.

A little has been done in this line with the help of UNRRA and other relief organisations. An education programme is underway in the camp and includes a nursery school, a school, a trade school and a flourishing theatre group, but materials and accommodation for these activities are most difficult to obtain, and the numbers catered for only touch a fringe of the camp population.

The theatre group is run by a former Berlin stage director who has spent the last seven years in twelve concentration camps but can still write and produce most excellent shows. These are performed in a drafty, leaky tent theatre, but casts and audience surmount such discomforts with immense enthusiasm.

The trade school runs classes in many subjects such as motor mechanics, dressmaking, carpentry and dental mechanics, but again lack of raw materials and tools is a serious handicap.

There is no possibility of employment for the mass of the people. There are a few keen, energetic and intelligent young people who find themselves work with the relief teams or local military government, but such openings are limited. There is little incentive to work, as money is practically of no value here, and there are no shops in Belsen in which to spend it. So those who work do so on an almost voluntary basis. I have had several remarkable young DPs helping me in my office and have thought what an asset they would be in any society.

One such girl, I have heard since I came home, has committed suicide. She was nineteen years old and had lost her entire family, which had been murdered by the Nazis. She had no connections overseas. She had wished to become a teacher and was wonderful with small children, but there seemed to be no future for her anywhere, and after having survived years in concentration camps she apparently could face life no longer.

I cannot forget Magda. Nor can I forget the other thousands who have as yet not given up hope but who still have a faith in the future—a future in a country where they can live like free people, where they can work, live and die like human beings. I think that only through generous emigration programmes in all countries where manpower is needed and where such people as these can make a vital and useful contribution to the community can the problem of Belsen be solved.

Memorial to those murdered in the Bergen-Belsen Concentration Camp, erected on the first anniversary of liberation

At the end of January I met Egon in Paris, and we went on to Grenoble, and he told me of his times there and of his work in the Maquis. We had ten days in Alp d'Huez, with beautiful skiing and much laughter. I remember standing at the top of a slope as Egon skied down very professionally and one of a young French couple standing beside me said 'Pas mal pour son age' (not bad for his age). I skied down and joined Egon, who enjoyed this remark. He had taken the door off a broken-down shed nearby, and we sat on it and ate our lunch, relaxed and happy, enjoying beautiful views, lovely snow and bright sunshine. Then we decided that we should get married when Egon got his summer leave and came to England.

AJDC offered to re-employ me if I returned to Germany after our wedding. There was still a great deal of work to do in Belsen; many people were still stuck there. Many of those who had returned to Poland and not found any family came back to Belsen in the hope of ultimately getting to Palestine, as did many from the harsh regimes in eastern Communist countries. The camp did not close until 1950, five years after the liberation.

Trip to New York

On my return to the UK I met my friend Doreen Lewisohn in London, and she told me that her father was trying to get her a passage to New York. I said rather jokingly, 'Do get me one, too. I have now earned some dollars and my uncle has always asked me to visit him in New York.' When I arrived in Belfast I received a message saying that Doreen's father had managed to secure two berths for us on the *Queen Elizabeth*, leaving the United Kingdom for New York in March. So I planned my first trip to the USA, going out by ship and flying back to Shannon Airport in Eire, to catch a train from Dublin to Belfast.

I spent three splendid weeks in America and had many adventures.

They started with my departure from Belfast, when a violent snowstorm struck Scotland. I travelled from Belfast to the port of Stranraer, to find that there were no trains coming up from London because the snow was so deep that all the traffic had been stopped. After waiting a day in Stranraer it was decided that the ship should go to Greenock, a port further south. We did this and found that the first train to get through from London had arrived there. We all packed onto this. Everybody became very friendly and chatty, and I mentioned that I was trying to get to London to go down to Southampton to catch the ship to America. I met a chap who offered to drive me to Southampton, but he alighted before reaching London.

First of all we stopped at a little station because there was no restaurant car on the train, and we piled out to buy a cup of tea, all except for some Air Force boys, who decided that they would prefer beer to station tea and went to a pub down the road. The whistle blew and the train was ready to depart, but the RAF missed it. Our compartment was piled high with kitbags, which were thrown out at the next station.

We reached Crewe and had a further stop, so that I was able to telephone my sister Helen (who was waiting for me) to make sure that the door to her block of flats would be kept open for me, since it was quite late. We arrived in London about midnight. I had planned to pick up a coat and skirt that were being made for me by my sister's tailor, but they were not finished in time for my journey.

The boat train left Victoria station at 9.00am the next day, and when I joined it my friend Doreen was already there, waiting anxiously and wondering whether I would turn up. We got down to Southampton in time to board the *Queen Elizabeth*.

Doreen and I shared a cabin with two other girls, each of whom had a small farewell gift on her bunk. My bunk was empty, but next morning I was told to expect a radio call at noon. When it came, it turned out to be my erstwhile Sir

Galahad from the train, checking to see if I had made it to the ship. This restored my self esteem, which had been damaged by the empty bunk on embarkation.

It was a rough voyage, and the ship hove to in mid-Atlantic to face the wind until the gale blew itself out and calmer waters returned. I had been induced to leave my bunk by Doreen, who insisted that I join her for the wonderful meals of food that had not been seen in England for many years.

My US holiday included a visit to Washington, where I saw the wonderful art galleries, and also a trip to upstate New York. Here Uncle Charlie had a charming small house called Hill Top Farm (which he left to his friend and long term partner Harry Footer in his will). Towards the end of my stay I received a cable from Egon, who was feeling neglected, not having received many letters, wanting to know if all was well with me. Charlie replied on my behalf: 'Unkraut verdirbt nicht' (weeds don't perish). All well, much love.'

I flew home via Dublin, then took the train back to Belfast with all my treasures—things such as a radio and nylon stockings, that were not yet available in the United Kingdom.

Marriage

I had planned to marry in Belfast, but when I learnt that marrying a 'stateless' person would rob me of my British nationality, Egon and I decided to marry in London. The Home Office had advised me that my application for naturalization could be processed there within a few days. Egon was insistent on this, as he would not let me take the risk of traveling through Europe as a stateless person. In July 1947 therefore I left Belfast and stayed with my sister Amélie in Highgate to await Egon's arrival in London, so that I could apply for my naturalization in order to get a British passport that would enable me to return to work in Belsen as Mrs Fink.

Egon arrived two or three days before 29 July, the day of our wedding. When I applied for a marriage license in Highgate I was asked how long Egon had been resident in the United Kingdom and I said that he had been here three days. I was informed that three weeks' residency was required. It did not suit us to wait for three weeks, so I transferred my application to the address of my sister Helen in Knightsbridge. This time I told a little white lie and said that Egon had been in England three weeks.

Egon had a friend in London who was his best man, and Helen was to come to the registry office as my witness. It was a very hot summer, and Egon had eaten something that was not quite fresh and had disagreed with him, and at the registry office they thought his agitation was a sign of nervousness and told him not to worry because it was a very simple ceremony. When Egon had to leave the room for a few minutes the man who was registering the marriage realized that he had made a mistake and that it was not nerves.

Outside the registry office there was a commercial photographer who insisted on taking our photographs. Then we retreated to the Rubens Hotel, where we had booked a table for lunch for Amélie and her husband Dixon, and Joan and Joan's daughter Sarah. Helen was there, of course, and Egon's best man. We had a nice meal, with champagne, and from there Egon and I took one of the tourist boats down the Thames as far as Greenwich, after which we took ourselves off for an evening meal. The next day Amélie invited many of my London friends to her garden in Highgate for tea. Professor Meredith, a Belfast professor friend of Amélie's with a long black beard and a bright orange shirt, was also there. One of my friends who came in thought that this was Egon and was greatly relieved when she found she had made a mistake.

Peggy and Egon on their wedding day, 29 July 1947, outside the Chelsea registry office

The next day we took the boat to Belfast and I was able to introduce Egon to my father. The old maid who looked after him very devotedly was looking down from the top of a landing and told me later on that she was so pleased to see that I had married a 'nice big fella'. She and Egon got on very well, as he did also with my father. At tea my father chatted to Egon, saying: 'How do you expect to keep my daughter at the standard of life to which she is accustomed?' Egon, not at all abashed, said: 'Well, Mr Loewenthal, I like a good standard of life myself and if I have one, Peggy will too'.

And so we spent a couple of days in Belfast and then took ourselves to a country cottage on the Antrim coast overlooking a very beautiful bay, miles from civilization. It was beautiful, restful and peaceful with nice summer weather. In the morning I noticed that Egon had found a shoebrush and to my great surprise was standing there polishing his shoes. This was the result of his training in the Foreign Legion, where he was used to having to keep his uniform spotless.

After five or six days in this secluded spot we took the car and motored south, where we again stayed in a cottage, in Newcastle, County Down. It was a lovely mountainous area overlooking the sea—very peaceful, with lovely flowers, and masses of wild fuchsia along the coast. Here a lot of friends came to visit and to meet Egon. The ten days or so we were there flew past, and then it was time for Egon to return to work. He left without me, as my naturalization had still not come through.

I had lost my nationality on marrying Egon, as in those days a wife took her husband's nationality. I couldn't prove that Egon was not an enemy alien, although he had fought with the Allies, firstly in the French Ski Troops, secondly in the Foreign Legion and finally in the Maquis, fighting the Nazis from the hills above Grenoble. Nor could I prove that he had been stripped of his Austrian citizenship, as he had no letters or papers to show this.

I had sent my papers to the Home Office before leaving London and now waited impatiently for my naturalization to come through. After six or eight weeks nothing had happened, and I finally decided that I could wait no longer; it was stupid to remain in the UK when I was a newly married woman with a husband in Germany and a job waiting for me there as well. So I left, and when I got to Dover, where there were two doors, one that read 'Foreigners—non-British' and the other 'British subjects', I went through the latter, using my valid passport in my maiden name.

Egon had come to Paris to meet me, and here there was difficulty again, because the organization had got me what was known as 'Call Forward Papers to Germany' in the name of Fink, and this document had to be stamped but it included no entry visa to allow me into France, so I was fined for illegal entry. (The organization later paid this fine.) Some months later I was called to the British consulate in Hamburg, where my passport was finally ready. The official obviously thought that I was not behaving properly, because I was told to take my hands out of my pockets, as this was a serious matter. After all, I had to swear allegiance to the monarch in order to become naturalized!

Peggy and Egon in 1947, outside GB3—the Belsen headquarters of the AJDC

And so we returned to Belsen. Here Egon had found us married accommodation in the gate lodge of the Glynn Hughes Hospital. There were two flats in this little building. The ground floor flat was occupied by good friends, Eva and Sasha Gottlieb, who were also newlyweds; he was a Polish doctor who had fought in the Royal Army Medical Corps and his wife had come from Berlin as one of the ten thousand unaccompanied children who had arrived in England in 1939. Sasha and Eva were a dear couple. They both worked for the English Jewish Organization, and ultimately they emigrated to Australia.

I got a warm welcome back from everyone and started working in the Emigration Department once more, trying to solve the problems for many Jewish DPs who were still anxious to get out of Germany and start a new life elsewhere. Most wanted to go to Palestine and to have a state of their own, which ultimately they got, in Israel.

One day the head of the Düsseldorf Jewish community came to Belsen to collect supplies. Egon was in charge of this department, and as Mr Goldberg arrived Egon said, 'Let me introduce you to my wife, Peggy', whereupon Mr Goldberg said: 'Ha ha, Fink! Whenever you are with a pretty girl you introduce her as your wife.' I said: 'This time, Mr Goldberg, it is quite kosher,' and I showed him my ring and we all laughed a great deal.

The Grynszpans on the train leaving Belsen
They were the parents of Hershel Feibel Grynszpan whose assassination of Nazi foreign service officer Ernst vom Rath in Paris on 7 November 1938 sparked off "Kristallnacht" on the night of 9–10 November 1938

There was much rejoicing in Belsen (now an entirely Jewish camp) when the state of Israel was established, and many DPs left for the new homeland. At the same time some of the Jewish DPs who had returned to Poland and found themselves under a Communist regime filtered back.

1947 was a very difficult year for Anglo-Jewry as the terrorist violence against the British authority in Palestine increased. Anti-British feeling was also prevalent in the camp. America was pressing for the creation of a Jewish state. There was also great difficulty between the various branches of the Jewish internees, with the orthodox and liberal Jews and the Zionists all giving voice to their differing desires.

I personally fell between these things. I was employed by the AJDC, which was the rich relation of all the Jewish relief units, and the rumblings of anti-British feeling were quite strong, so my emotions and loyalties were divided between being British and being an employee of the Americans working for the DPs.

An elderly couple called Grynspan were among the first transport leaving for Israel by train from the nearby station. It was their son Herschel who in 1940 had shot and killed the Nazi German consul in the German embassy in Paris, revenge for which had culminated in Kristallnacht—the burning of all synagogues in Germany and then the rounding up of Jews and the smashing of Jewish shop windows and the plundering of Jewish shops.

Later in the year Egon and I made a trip to Marseille, as the Jewish Agency were working there trying to arrange shipping for the people on their way to Israel. In his youth Egon had spent a holiday in Morocco, and he was anxious to see what was happening there, as Moroccan Jews were now filtering through, hoping to get to the promised land.

Our stay in Marseille was really very pleasant, and I enjoyed some lovely meals along the coast. The weather was beautiful and sunny, and everything was luxurious compared to our normal living standards.

AJDC headquarters were considering starting a program in Morocco and thought that Egon should go there on their behalf.

Morocco: 1948–1957

AJDC in Morocco

Although Camp 2 was closed only in 1950, most of the DPs there had emigrated in 1948, after the British left Palestine and the Jewish state of Israel began to settle down. It was at the end of this year that Egon and I, after a home leave in the United Kingdom, left for Morocco. Jews had settled in North Africa following the expulsion of Jews from Spain in 1492, and it was for the descendants of these people that AJDC decided to run a medical and educational program so that would-be emigrants to Israel would be in a better condition medically and educationally.

The poverty in the French colony was extreme for both Arabs and Jews. The Alliance Israélite, a French Jewish relief organization, had been working for many years in Morocco, and there were some 24,000 schoolchildren being helped by them. Many suffered from both ringworm of the scalp and blindness as the result of trachoma. These conditions were dirt-related and very prevalent, results of the low standard of living.

En route to Morocco we stayed in the Hotel Deux Mondes in Paris, which was small but comfortable. In the evenings we ate our dinner in a nearby little restaurant and drank our bottle of rosé d'Anjou. Egon was getting details of his job as assistant director from the AJDC's headquarters. We then took the train to Marseille and from there a boat to Casablanca.

From the rails of the ship I watched our approach into the port and saw hundreds of busy Arabs carting loads and sacks on their backs, and donkey carts with crates and goods of all sorts being unloaded; these hundreds of people were milling around in brown and white jellabas (or nightgowns, as I called them). Strange, exciting smells and a bright blue sky greeted us as we finally arrived at the hotel. It was owned by a Jewish Moroccan who had made a successful livelihood, having started as a boy selling bottles of paraffin oil out of an old pram. He was now a worthy citizen, helping to alleviate the poverty of the local Jewish population.

There was already an AJDC office in the town, run by two local ladies, Mme Benjio and Nellie Benater. Egon was the first overseas assistant director to arrive; later an American director joined us. Our first job was finding somewhere to live, and with the help of Mme Benjio we found a furnished villa owned by a Mme Levi. It was rather large and set in a walled garden. The rooms were big and had a lot of velvet curtains—very dark and heavy for this hot climate. There was a garage in which an Arab gardener lived with several children.

Some months after our arrival Egon was chairing a meeting and had to introduce the speaker, Mme Benater, who was a rather plump elderly lady. His opening phrase was unfortunate, referring to 'our good friend Belly Nenatur'!

The poorer Jewish population lived in a part of the town known as the Mellah, a mass of dark, crowded dwellings with very little sanitation and very great poverty. The Arabs lived in a different area, known as the Bidonville, which represented another side of the town, equally poverty-stricken. The country was still ruled by the French when we arrived, and there was a great deal of national pressure on them to get out, with occasional bombings and other terrorist activities. The Moroccans of course gradually gained their freedom.

At the beginning of our stay in Casablanca we heard of a quarter called Bousbierre. This had been set up by the early French settlers, and the name of a captain Prospère turned into Bousbierre. It was a brothel area for the troops, and many girls went there to earn a marriage allowance. Before they could find husbands they had to have a dowry. This area was controlled by the French, and the girls had to pass a medical checkpoint. Certain evenings were for the navy, others for the military, but if any visitors came just because they were intrigued, or if someone came with a woman, the girls knew that it was not a 'business meeting' but only a floor show. On several occasions we took visiting Americans to see Bousbierre. This was one of our earliest experiences; soon after our arrival it was closed down.

In the house I had a Jewish woman, Hannah, from the Mellah, who came in the mornings to help me with preparing food and cleaning the house. Once a week I had a nice Arab woman, Tamo, from the Bidonville, who came to do the washing. This was done in a cellar with cold water and bleach, all rather primitive. Tamo and Hannah got on extremely well together, and on feast days, either Jewish or Arab, they would arrive with little bunches of flowers for each other. Seeing such examples of friendly coexistence, it was very sad to hear how the politicians would bring the people to such disastrous disagreement over race and religion.

Being pregnant, I decided in September 1949 to go back to London for the birth, because a child born in Morocco might have difficulty with British citizenship, and also because hospitals in Morocco were very unsatisfactory and unreliable. I was able to fly back to London in a mildly pregnant state a few months before Michelle was born. Not having done much flying previously, I was very impressed and had a wonderful journey. Egon had obtained for me a good seat on French Airlines, which had a wonderful menu.

This also gave me a chance to go back to Belfast for a month and see my father, who was getting on in years. I had made arrangements to have Michelle in a London hospital. I was not the youngest of mothers, and Amélie, my medical sister, thought it advisable for me to go to University College Hospital. After my short stay in Belfast I went to stay with Amélie in Highgate till Michelle's arrival. When she was born, on 29 January 1950, Jossel Rosensaft from Belsen, who was now settled in New York, arrived with a large bunch of white lilacs to congratulate me. The concept of being able to obtain lilac in January in itself was impressive!

A few days after the birth the young obstetrician visited me, saying in a very matter-of-fact manner that Michelle was being x-rayed, as there was a swelling on the side of her head about which they were concerned. He asked me whether there was any history of congenital problems in the family. Horrified and shocked and in floods of tears, I rang my sister, who promised to ask her husband Dixon, who was Professor of Anatomy at the London hospital, to contact my consultant. The consultant explained that the x-ray had been taken, showing an unusual hole on the side of the skull which he thought might have resulted from the forceps delivery. Dixon, however, assured the consultant that this would close without consequence, as does the fontanelle. Indeed this was so. The next morning the consultant visited me, remarking: 'I did not know you had an eminent brother-in-law!'

After a couple of weeks I flew back to Belfast to await Egon's arrival, but he had not been able to leave the job when he had hoped to, as various emergencies had arisen. In fact it was a couple of months before he got home leave to meet his daughter. I remember being very impressed when I saw him one evening taking off his shoes and creeping towards the room where the baby slept, just to go and have a look at her.

When this precious baby was about two and a half months old we made plans to return to Casablanca, and as conditions there were still fairly primitive I decided to invest in a nanny to come with me in case I developed flu or met with some difficulty in caring for Michelle. I finally found Gwendoline Wright in the Nursery World, and she came to see me and turned out to be very efficient.

Peggy at Lennoxvale with Michelle, February 1950

Egon named her "Schnurbart Franzl" because she had quite a nice little moustache (schnurbart being German for moustache). She was somewhat younger than I was but had had lots of experience with babies and was a great standby; I did not want her to take over the job of caring for Michelle but just to take on the 'nasty bits'. She was prepared to cope with difficulties such as water shortages (water was in rather short supply in Casablanca, and we were liable to be cut off from ten in the morning until five in the afternoon).

The staff in the Casablanca office had increased considerably, to one social worker, several people looking after the schools, an American medical doctor, Dr Raphael, with his family and another assistant to Egon. They all had children and we all became very good friends.

Peggy, Michelle and Egon c.1952

One of Egon's jobs was to visit the countryside and, with help from the Jewish Agency, try to make a rough estimate of the condition of the Jewish population in Morocco as a whole and to assess to what extent the number of would-be emigrants to Israel would be likely to increase.

One day a young man came to the office to ask Egon for supplies for his community, which was far out on the borders of the desert. Egon thought he recognized him, and it turned out they had met in the Foreign Legion. The young man had joined up by lying about his age to the French Army, and Egon, seeing that he was so young and was having a very hard life, had protected him in camp and eventually got him returned to his home town. At first the young man was amazed when Egon told him that they had met before during the war, but then he remembered the incident of his return home to his parents.

We went back to our rather large cheerless house. Egon had got into the habit of trying to teach the gardener how to wash his children and how to write or count a little, but poor Ahmed did not make much progress. I thought it was awful to have someone living in the garage until I saw how most of the people lived in the slums and what luxury it was to be near a tap with water. I think they went to fields up the road, as there was no toilet for his family.

We did not stay in this house very long but decided to invest in something more modern, and after much searching we found a small bungalow in 19 Rue Languedoc, one of the roads slightly out of town. This little house had three bedrooms and a bathroom and one living/dining room and a small kitchen, with 'Butagas' (bottled gas, here was no gas laid on in those days). It was quite adequate and had a nice little garden. The front of the house was built over a garage, but the back of the house was the ground floor, as the house was built on a slope. Here we had a very nice home.

I did my voluntary work with my committee and Michelle finally went to a nearby kindergarten. Through the school I got to know more people and managed to make many new friends. Michelle was speaking both French and English at this time. I remember when she, aged three and a half or four, had to interpret for the headmistress when an American father wanted to register his child. There was a certain amount of unrest during the struggle for independence, and frequently the kindergarten was locked for fear that some of the children might be taken as hostages.

Gradually there was a gentle flow of emigrants from Morocco to Israel. The emigration was handled by the Jewish Agency, working in close contact with the Joint (AJDC).

I remember various events in our daily life. One morning Egon left to inspect a depot where the stores were kept. He had built up a storehouse and appointed a local manager and staff, and he tried to impress on the employees that there was no smoking in this area. This morning as he came in to the storehouse he saw one of the workboys with a cigarette. He got very cross with this poor lad and struck a packing case hard with his fist, saying: 'How often do I have to tell you no smoking means no smoking?' On the case above there was a pot of red paint, which was knocked off by the great thump and came down on Egon's shoulder, leaving large streaks of red paint on his sports jacket. In an even worse temper, he left the storehouse and drove back to change his clothes, but I was looking out of the window when he returned and got a terrible shock when I saw my husband with what appeared to be blood-soaked arms! Later Mr Ansalon, who was in charge of the employees, arrived at our home bringing a jacket length of tweed to replace the ruined garment.

Then there was our first burglar. Poor Nursie, as the nanny was then called, slept in a room on the ground floor of the bungalow and, being a good English lady, she liked to have her window open at night, not fearing any mishap. She was awakened one night by the creaking door of the wardrobe at the foot of her bed. When she switched on the light there was an Arab who I think was as frightened as she was, because on seeing her he took a leap, jumped out the window and fled. However, she, poor girl, was utterly shattered, especially as this good fellow had collected some bits that he had found which he thought he would like and had left them on a chair in a scarf, and these included a very dangerous curved Arab knife in a sheath that she had bought on the market square. After this she slept with her windows tightly closed and shuttered.

Some months later I was sleeping on a divan underneath our big window because Egon had a bad cold. This window consisted of a large central window with a small one on each side. One of the small ones was open, but this was at the end of the house that was over the garage, so it was quite high off the ground. I woke up to feel the cover slipping off the foot of my bed. There was some light coming through the window, and when I looked there was a chap crouched in the window with one foot on my bed, just entering the room. I jumped out of bed; he took flight through that small window, and I almost came face to face with him as he clung to the ladder that he had placed against the wall. I had a quick thought that if I pushed him he might break his neck. I didn't want that, but while I paused he was down the ladder and away.

I woke Egon, saying: 'There's an Arab trying to get in!' whereupon he said: 'Do you want me to be a hero in pyjamas?' Finally I got him out of bed and, as we really didn't wish poor Nursie to have a heart attack, we removed the ladder, brought it into the hall and shut the window, intending to remove the ladder early in the morning so that she would not know. She heard us, however, and we told her the story. Later, going around the house, we found there was a crate in the corner which the burglar had used to get over the wall into the neighbour's garden. Subsequently, with new bars on the windows, we had no more burglar trouble.

One evening when Egon and I were taking a stroll in town we passed a modern shop full of electrical equipment, and amongst the brightly lit items was a large brown rat sitting up washing his whiskers with his paws. This seemed to us to be a perfect illustration of the state of the country at that time. There were small Arab children sleeping over gratings in the main shopping street from which a little heat from the workrooms below the surface of the street might escape, and I felt very bad returning to my house and finding my child tucked in her cot with clean sheets and knowing that she had all the food and care that was necessary.

After a rainy period when there were pools of water on the street there would be a trickle of olive oil floating on the surface, and I frequently saw women from the Mellah scooping this little bit of oil up into a jar to use for their food.

I no longer worked for AJDC after Michelle was born, but I started a voluntary committee to back up the medical social worker of the Organisation Secours aux Enfants (OSE), whose dispensary was now established near the Mellah. We met weekly to discuss problem cases that were presented to us. The medical social worker affirmed that the exchange of ideas helped her to solve many of her difficulties. We established a depot for clothing distribution, distribution of food parcels, assistance for the blind and for the deaf and dumb, assistance for backward children who were treated at a special clinic, and cash relief. We also studied applications for a nursery school that had been opened by OSE.

Our committee consisted of local, more affluent, Jewish ladies and was generously backed by AJDC, and we also collected a considerable amount of money locally. The social workers were following some 350 cases each month; the conditions in the Mellah were deplorable. There were families with miniscule incomes living in abject poverty, often in one dark room with no windows or running water. Cases of children who were maimed by polio were frequently mentioned, and there were many blind children, all suffering from malnutrition. Any help provided made a great deal of difference to these unfortunate people.

The first and much needed deaf and dumb school in North Africa was started in Casablanca by a young woman who had been trained in France. This was arranged by our committee.

In the political unrest at this time, as the Arabs revolted against French occupation, the Jewish population was considered second class citizens. The annual budget of our little committee had grown from 1,800 francs in 1951 to 1,260,104 francs in 1955. We did get some satisfaction from knowing that we were able to provide a little help to this poverty-stricken population.

The Anfa Hotel was a large and elegant hotel in a fine garden with palm trees and flower beds on the outskirts of Casablanca. In the spring the countryside near the sea was very lovely, with a blue cloudless sky and masses of wild orange marigolds. It was in this hotel that Churchill, Stalin and Roosevelt held their conference at the end of World War II.

We frequently went to a nearby little wood ("le petit bois") with Michelle and her friends and their parents for picnics under the shade of the evergreen trees. We made other outings, sometimes to the racecourse, and once when we were watching a horse race Michelle, aged about five, asked: 'Which horse wins, the horse that comes first or the last one?'

I remember once when we were driving through the country and there was a swarm of locusts. They were clinging to the telegraph wires and devouring any greenery available. One of these creatures flew into the back of the car where Michelle sat and there was a great cry of horror. When I assured her that the insect could not harm her, she replied: 'Oh, but it has such an ugly and unfriendly face!' The Moroccans roasted locusts on charcoal stoves and they were thought to be a great delicacy.

There were many other Jewish relief agencies as well as the Joint working in Morocco. One that was doing a training program and occupational education for the young was ORT (a world organization devoted to education, which began in Russia; the name is an acronym for the original Russian name). There was also OSE, doing medical work. One young man who was working with ORT confided to me at a party one day that he was having a problem because he had fallen in love with a local Jewish girl who was very much his junior and he didn't know what he should do. I suggested that he should propose to her and if they did not have a family at once and disagreed they could then separate. Much later I heard that Victor Smarga had moved with his wife to the Geneva headquarters and that they had two little girls.

Very many years later, when I was in Geneva with Egon at an AJDC annual meeting, we were strolling down the main shopping street, Rue du Rhone, past all the fashionable shops, when we came to two little bay trees in pots on either side of a large doormat at the entrance to one of the most elegant shops. On this mat was written "A.S.", and in the window was an antique chest with an Yves St Laurent scarf draped over it in one corner and a very expensive outfit in the other. Our companion announced that this was Anita Smarga's establishment. I don't know whether she was still married to Victor, but she had started this dress shop with a friend who had helped her to sew clothes for her two little daughters when they first arrived in Geneva, and it was now one of the foremost fashion houses in the city. I never managed to contact her.

In the spring of 1952 Egon and I had a short holiday on our own, leaving Michelle in the care of faithful Nursie, backed up by a French friend who was also working with AJDC. We drove in our Austin A40 to Tangiers, then to Gibraltar, visiting Seville, Cordova and Grenada, all very lovely and interesting. Having telephoned to hear that all was well in 19 Rue Languedoc, we had a most enjoyable and relaxing time.

Later that summer Michelle, Nursie and I escaped from the heat of Morocco and went to France with another French AJDC couple, Henri and Anne Laufer, and their child Danielle, who was a little younger than Michelle. Egon joined us later and we toured in the old Austin. I now remember little about this excursion except that once when Egon took a photograph of Michelle, telling her to sit down and say cheese, she asked him to take a snap also of Danielle, whom she instructed in French to sit down and say 'fromage'.

We stopped in Geneva, where Nursie left us to return to the United Kingdom. I got letters from her annually for the next forty-five years.

I had kept in touch with a young Viennese woman, Hedy Kerpen, who had escaped Hitler in 1939 by going to Belfast, and I asked her if she would care to spend a year with us in Casablanca. Conditions were still a little primitive in Morocco, and I felt I would like to have a backup from Britain in case I were unwell. So Hedy flew to Geneva and joined us. We returned to Casablanca at the end of the summer of 1952 via Lyons, Orange and Marseilles, whence we took the boat back to Morocco.

Our life in Morocco continued smoothly. We were now settled in our little house in Rue Languedoc, Michelle happily so in nursery school. My Jewish house-help, Hannah, had emigrated to Israel, as had many of the employees at AJDC and the other organizations, to escape from the poverty of Casablanca. I had Fatima to take Hannah's place.

Egon had taken many journeys into the interior of the country with Jewish Agency members, trying to assess approximate numbers of would-be emigrants to Israel. When these people were asked their ages, some of the replies would be vague. Born in the year of the flash floods, born in the year of the last locust plague. Education was minimal, but the desire to lead a better life was universal.

When we visited Marrakesh, we stayed in the Mamounia Hotel, where Churchill spent his painting holidays. This was close to the huge square, the Place Djemaa el Fna, where all day and late into the night hundreds of little stalls sold all sorts—silverware, sweetmeats, leather and many other things—and locusts and kebabs were cooked on charcoal stoves. There were snake charmers with cobras writhing out of baskets to the sound of a flute, and storytellers sitting cross-legged on the ground. The dentist sat on a stool with his patient on the ground, his head between the knees of the dentist, who waved aloft the offending tooth in large pliers. There were music-makers, dancers, fortune tellers etc., and in the background the high snow-covered Atlas mountains. And always masses of people, who came from the hills nearby and the smaller towns, pushing and crowding.

One wealthy trader, El-Kaeem, whose family had made its wealth trading salt, which was carried by camels into the desert, lived close by in Marrakesh. He was the chairman of the local Jewish community, and invited us into his family's house. The house was built around an interior square patio, with the same living quarters on the ground floor as on the first floor. In winter the family lived upstairs, since the heat rose, and in the summer it was cooler on the ground floor. I shall always remember the meals we had with them, my plate piled high with all sorts of sweetmeats in spite of my protests, and very sweet mint tea served as a beverage.

We visited many towns in Morocco, including the beautiful city of Fez. A long time ago this was a seat of learning. Here also leather goods were made. In the tanneries there were great vats where the skins were soaked in different tubs of many colours, boys standing and stamping in these tubs with their bare legs to mix the leather and the colours. The streets, which were covered with matting, were narrow and twisting—souks full of stalls on either side, selling leather goods, silver hand-made jewellery and many other things.

It was colourful and busy. There were also stalls with clothing, and at the back of these stalls you would see very tiny children sitting in the shade, crossing and re-crossing their hands. They were making the braid to put along the edges of jellabas and spent all day so employed.

One of the other towns was Mazagan, on the coast. The Portuguese overran these areas many years ago, and in Mazagan there was a tremendous cistern for underground water catchment, full of strange arches and wonderful architecture. A film of *Othello* was once made there. The town also had its French quarter, as did all the towns under French occupation.

Mogador was a coastal port where the family Belisha originated. It was Hoare Belisha who introduced the Belisha beacon pedestrian crossings. It was said that his family shipped their laundry home to England to be done, and it was then shipped back again to Morocco.

Rabat, where the government of Morocco was set up, was a large French town planned by Lyautey when he governed Morocco as a French province. After the liberation Moulet Hassan had his palace there. He was Pasha and king of Morocco.

It was said that the story of Robinson Crusoe originated in Saffi, another coastal town.

Further south was Agadir; this is now a large tourist area, though there was a very bad earthquake in the town in the 1960s. We had a very amusing incident there when we once drove down for a day. It was a long drive along the coast to get to the beautiful sandy beaches of Agadir. One of the party was Dennis Hamson, the husband of my doctor in Casablanca, Lucy Hamson, who had gone to England for a holiday, leaving him in charge of two bull terriers, one of which she had been advised by the vet was suffering from a false pregnancy. This dog was shut in the back of Dennis' car, in a shady place with the windows open. When we returned to the car with some water for her, to his horror he found five puppies. He was very cross with his wife for leaving him in a situation where he had to return on his own to Casablanca to look after his canine family.

While in Marrakesh, we visited a village called Asru in the hills of the Atlas mountains. Here we were invited into a peasant's house built of mud, wattle and reeds. The family lived on the first floor; underneath were the donkeys and the chickens. To get to the first floor, one had to climb a ladder made of a tree trunk from which the branches on either side had been cut off to make steps. Sitting crosslegged on the roof, which swayed slightly (it was made of dried mud between palm branches), we were served little glasses of very sweet mint tea. It was a strange experience.

At Easter in 1955, when Michelle was five, we went for a holiday with friends to another little town, also in the foothills of the Atlas mountains. This town was called Ifrane, and here there was still a patch of snow on the slopes. This was Michelle's first sight and experience of snow. It was a very beautiful valley, and we enjoyed the time with several of our friends from AJDC.

Most summers in Morocco were extremely hot, so Michelle and I generally escaped. Egon came with us when he was able to get away from his work. In 1953 we acquired an amazing Alvis car. The Pasha had ordered two Alvis cars through a garage in Casablanca but had accepted only one of them, thus leaving the garagiste with a large car on his hands. Egon fell in love with it, and the garage was very glad to get rid of it at a reduced price.

In 1953 we set off from Casablanca for Bordeaux in this car, and then we went on to Paris, London and Cambridge. Egon later returned to Morocco, and Michelle and I joined my sister Amélie with her four small boys at the seaside in Wales. After some time a flu bug infected Michelle; she was in bed, and just about the time we were due to return to Cambridge I caught it, so my sister took Michelle with her family back to Cambridge while I waited for my high temperature to disappear.

Michelle and I had been boarding in a very primitive little boarding house with no electricity and only oil lamps in the bedrooms. I was looked after by an Indian doctor, who after several days decided that I should go into hospital. I arrived at a Nissen hut establishment that was the local hospital in Haverford West, and a few days later had been cured and was able to return to the family. In the meantime some of the good ladies in the ward were very surprised when I was able to get up and take my turn at the tea trolley. One of them remarked: 'We never thought you would be so friendly. When you came in you looked so cross.' I had had a temperature of 103 and was not feeling at all jolly or matey when I went in! From Cambridge we returned to join Egon at the end of the summer.

The following summer, 1954, Michelle and I escaped the heat again and traveled on a Japanese cargo boat. This was also an interesting experience. There was a crew of twenty or thirty and some six passengers. One evening, sitting with one of the officers at our meal table, I admired a Japanese teapot with a rush handle, saying that I would very much like to buy one. I was told that these things were not for sale, but the night we docked in London I found on my bunk, with the compliments of the captain, this beautiful teapot, which I still have in Cambridge today.

On this holiday Michelle and I went to visit my friends in Ireland, the Kohners, and I had to have an operation and was able to leave Michelle with my friends, who had rented a house on the coast outside Belfast. We returned in September by plane to join Egon in Morocco.

In the summer of 1955 we had another adventure. The famous Alvis needed to be serviced, and as nobody knew anything about such a car in Casablanca, Michelle and I once again took a Japanese cargo boat—this time with a friend—now sailing to Southampton, whence I had to drive this enormous object up to London and leave it in a garage there. I did not dare to drive through London, so I rang up the garage and a driver came to pick us up on the outskirts of the city.

Egon joined us later, and on our return we traveled via Ostend, through Brussels and down to Austria. Coming through Germany we were driving very fast on the motorway. When we came to Chiemsee we decided to spent the night there. It was getting dark, and Egon took the car from the front of the hotel after Michelle and I had got out. As he drove gently round to the parking lot the steering seemed faulty. We had a mechanic look at it, and he found that the steering rod had broken. It was very lucky that it had not happened in the afternoon when we were traveling at high speed on the motorway. It was several days before we could get the missing part; it had to be flown out from England, as these Alvis cars were not widely distributed across Europe. However, we moved on some days later and arrived in Austria and then on to Grenoble, where Egon's half-brother Poldi lived, and finally down to Marseille and home at the beginning of October. That was a long leave.

While in Morocco Egon received a decoration from the Sultan of Marocco (Chevalier Ouissam Aloaouite) for social service.

Vienna: 1957–1971

Vienna

The political situation in Europe at this time was rather disturbing. In 1956–57 the Russians had entered Budapest and the refugee problem began again. This time people were trying to get out from behind the Iron Curtain to Austria, and many refugee centres were set up near Vienna. In April 1957 we heard that we were needed in Vienna, so we were once again on the move. Egon went ahead of us to find a place to live while Michelle and I started to pack up our house in Rue Languedoc. For our final week in Casablanca Michelle and I stayed with Danish friends (the Moellers) whose son Eric was of one of Michelle's school friends.

As I got packed up and got the movers in to take our furniture I remember the Arab boys packing up everything and my saying to them: 'Now if it doesn't all go in, I do want that nice leather armchair to come with us.' Coming home from getting the papers in town I saw that everything had been packed except the armchair, and with all their pressing and squashing it would just not go in, so it remained to cover our telephone bill. Michelle and I took the plane for Vienna.

I remember Egon waiting for us at the other side of Customs and Michelle, not very old, running across without going through Customs shouting very loudly: 'Daddy, Daddy, guess what I've got in my rucksack. We have cigarettes for you!' Luckily, however, no one seemed to be much concerned about this smuggling effort.

Egon had been searching hard to find us a home. He had been helped by a young Hungarian woman, Poetty, who had been interned in Belsen at the age of sixteen and after liberation had married a Viennese, Alex Hirschl, also a refugee, with Egon acting as best man. They had returned to Vienna to reclaim his father's factory. Poetty had gone round many flats and houses with Egon, trying to choose the best one.

The flat they chose was in a large old house on the outskirts. It had a nice garden, and there were two bedrooms, a living room, a kitchen, and a bathroom with curtains instead of a door. It served its purpose well and the landlady, Maud Engelhardt, who lived upstairs, was very kind and helpful. She confessed that she had been a little puzzled by Egon and the pretty young 'Schatzi' who was helping him find our new home.

There was a French lycée in Vienna, so Michelle was able to start school straight away. Egon had again to establish an office, as many Hungarians were getting out from Budapest, where the Russians had taken over completely and the Communists were in charge.

There were other sister organizations working in Vienna at this time: the Catholic Welfare Council, the Quakers, the Red Cross and many others. Camps were set up for people who came through. Later on, following the fall of Dubcek in 1968, many Czechs fled, as did some Romanians, all washing up in and near Vienna, all without homes, moving on to different countries. Some time after this Russia permitted Jews to emigrate to Israel, and these people came through Vienna and were cared for by the Jewish Agency.

Once again we had to discuss the idea of obtaining a permanent home and not always living in rented accommodation, so my job was to investigate what was available. There had not been much building since the end of the war and I looked at many flats and houses. Nothing was very suitable or attractive, and all were very expensive.

There was a small piece of ground next to where we were living which had a large walnut tree and a view of the sloping vineyards on the edge of the Vienna Woods. This plot was owned by a Frau Hyek and her two sons, one a Professor of Anatomy at Vienna University, the other a well-known economist in the United States. I had friends who knew the family (Erwin Schroedinger, a famous physicist, who, with his wife, had escaped to Dublin just before the Anschluss; they had returned to Vienna some years after the war ended). There was a further link, as the professor's son knew of my brother-in-law who was Professor of Anatomy in Cambridge.

With this introduction I made an appointment with Frau Hyek to enquire about the land. She told me that she was willing to sell the property but her son in the USA would need to have his share paid in dollars. The price she mentioned was normal for the time, and the dollar payment presented no problem, as Egon could have his salary in US dollars. Thus we became the owners of this small, attractively situated but no longer cultivated vineyard.

Then came the problem of finding an architect. My sister Helen had known a Viennese architect, but he was now a professor of architecture at Harvard. She contacted him and he gave us the name of his colleague in Vienna, Professor Sep Stein, who became a close friend. After much discussion and deliberation he drew up plans for our first real home.

Our new home had to be attached to the large old pre-war building in which we were then living, as the end of this house came to the edge of our plot, and building regulations were such that we had to construct a semi-detached house. Sep's plans proved successful and we had a two storey house with balconies along the front at both levels, and cellars that gave us a garage and laundry and store rooms.

Egon, Peggy, Michelle and Schnuffi the dog at home in Vienna, c.1960

On the ground floor was an L-shaped living/dining room with a fireplace—which was unusual in Austria—adjoining a small study. At the back a good-sized kitchen where we ate when on our own, looking over our small garden with the lovely, shady old walnut tree and small paddling pool for Michelle. Upstairs were two small rooms with a shower in between, with delightful views of the hills. In front were two large bedrooms, one en suite, and with a dressing room between them.

We moved into No. 8 Amalgergasse in 1959 and spent happy years there until Egon's death in 1971.

I soon found some voluntary work to do. The Americans who worked at the embassy and other international organizations ran a thrift shop, selling clothing and other unneeded goods, partly for charity with a proportion for the owners. This took up one or two days a week, and through this shop I made many good friends. Egon made contact with many of these people in diplomatic work he was doing at the office.

Life in Austria was busy and satisfying, with a wonderful spread of activities that had not been available for the last ten years in Morocco. The countryside was beautiful, and we had many friends from all over the world. The International Atomic Energy Agency centre was in Vienna, and Egon worked in close connection with the US embassy. The museums and galleries, opera and orchestras were world famous. Smaller cultural activities were plentiful and easily available. Many friends and relatives visited us.

Peggy and Egon on skiing holiday in Saalbach, c.1960

We were able to have happy winter holidays skiing in Saalbach, a small village where we were joined by friends and their children.

Early in 1963 Egon was asked by the United Jewish Appeal—a fundraising organization covering all the American states—to go on a speaking tour of the USA to describe the overseas work of the AJDC. He turned out to be a very popular and successful speaker and was asked to go on several tours during the following years. On these tours he met many of the emigrants from Belsen who were now successfully established in America.

Later, in 1963, when Michelle was thirteen, we made our first trip to Israel, where Egon's half-brother Ernst and family were settled. We were shown much of this new and fast-growing country. In one developing new town, Ashdod, on the coast, large blocks of flats were being constructed and some small bungalows were built. Egon asked who lived there and could we visit one. He was told that a schoolteacher lived in one and we went in, discovering there a young man we recognized as the organizer of the temporary school in the Belsen DP camp, who gave us a great welcome.

When I was walking in Jerusalem a tall man stopped me in the street saying: 'Peggy, what are you doing here?' I did not at first recognize the Polish Dr Festing, who had organized the Belsen dispensary. He had been liberated in 1945 after several years of internment and was now married to an army doctor.

We also visited a new settlement for recent arrivals, where we met Rachael and her family. She had been the cleaner in AJDC's Casablanca office. She showed us with pride her three-roomed flat, saying she had been given an icebox, a table and chairs, beds, cooking pots and a brush 'all to keep Monsieur Fink'. She had lived in the miserable slums of Casablanca. Now her husband was working and her children were in schools. We were taken to an artists' colony in the hills where, in a cemetery, Egon recognized two old beggars at the gate asking for alms, just as they had done in Casablanca. We visited Tiberius and the Lake of Galilee, saw magnificent mosaics and swam in the Dead Sea. Here in Michelle's diary she wrote: 'Über al ist schön aber zu Haus am schönsten' (everywhere is beautiful, but home is best).

Our holiday plans for 1964 were cancelled, as I had slipped and fallen in our house and broken my hip. I went to the large public hospital, the Allgemeine Krankenhaus, as the consultant who was to operate was covering there full time over the summer and not seeing any private patients. The hospital had been built by Franz Josef in the last century and had not changed a lot! The operation was, however, splendid, and good results ensued, though the food was abysmal. I remember in particular one meal called 'grenadier march', which consisted of noodles and reheated cold potatoes.

The staff of the hospital were kept very busy at weekends by a large number of patients being admitted as a result of accidents caused by drunken drivers. The fresh wine made from grapes grown in the vineyards surrounding Vienna was very potent and sold by the owners in the many Heurigen bars and restaurants. These were pleasant places in which to spend a summer evening. Some were elegant establishments, others simple bars with cold meat snacks, often in the suburbs or in the Vienna woods.

One poor lady in my ward had her head and neck in plaster. She had a broken neck, having been in her Klapbett (a bed that folded up against the wall) when it accidentally folded up with her in it! Luckily my hip mended well, as did my next three broken hips (one in London and two in Cambridge) and my subsequent hip replacement.

AJDC had teams working in many European countries, and there were directors' meetings most years in various capitals. In 1965 I went to the Rome meeting with Egon, a lovely visit which I much enjoyed. I explored many old churches and in the evenings I would take Egon to the most interesting, until he said with exhaustion, 'I really can't look at any more holy families', so we would go and have a good meal instead. In 1966 Egon was again on a fund-raising trip in the US, and in the summer my sister Amélie and our friend Doreen Lewisohn joined us for a holiday in Korčula, on the Dalmatian coast of Yugoslavia, a very happy time.

By 1967 Michelle's schooling was over, and Egon had told her that when her exams were successfully finished he would take her on a trip (Maturareise), as was the custom in Austria. He said she could choose where she wanted to go, thinking that it might be somewhere like Paris or Florence. That summer, however, the world exhibition was in Montreal (Expo '67), and when Michelle had passed her Baccalauréat (mention bien) she suggested that they should go to Canada. This they did, flying home via the United States. This was a very good experience for both father and daughter. I went to London to meet them on their return.

Michelle spent six months in Cambridge, staying with a doctor and his family. She took classes at the Technical College (A level), applied for university entrance and was accepted (without any A level exams) by three universities. She chose a place at the University of East Anglia for October 1968, to study cell biology and genetics, and finished a BSc with Upper Second Class Honours in 1971.

In the late summer of 1967 my niece Sarah Day (Joan's daughter) came to visit us and we all planned to go on a short visit to Yugoslavia. Egon had to meet a VIP first, and we were waiting for him to return from the office when a telephone call came through saying that the VIP, an AJDC director who was inspecting the Prague programs, had been found assassinated in the river Moldau. He had left his hotel to buy a newspaper and had never returned. Charlie Jordan must, I think, have worked also for the

SIS. At this time there were many Communist troubles in Eastern European countries. We did eventually take our planned trip with Sarah.

Dubcek fell in 1968, and the flow of refugees from behind the Iron Curtain continued.

In February 1969 Egon once more had to do a speaking tour in the US, and, as Michelle was now at university in the UK, I was able to go with him. I stayed on Long Island with a friend from Casablanca, Belinde Aftalion, then crossed to a cousin's in San Francisco, Fred Lenway, where I met up with Egon so we could fly home together. We had an interesting and happy trip.

In June 1969, with Michelle still at university, Egon and I had three days in Budapest, going by river speedboat even more quickly than by car. This was my first visit to this beautiful town.

Michelle returned for the summer vacation, and she and I went with friends to Korčula, but Egon was unable to join us, as there was a flow of refugees out of Poland coming through Vienna.

It was about this time that Egon had a blood test and was found to have an acute exacerbation of his chronic myeloid leukaemia for which he had been treated since 1963. He had been feeling tired and had had a spell in hospital, where he was said to be 'stabilised', but he continued to work, going to the office for half days. He was not well enough to go to Michelle's graduation from the University of East Anglia in Norwich, but Amélie was there. When she graduated in 1971 Michelle decided to take the offer of a job in the Vienna Cancer Research Institute.

She knew of Egon's illness but was quite upset to find him in such a poor state on her return. In July he died suddenly but peacefully in our house.

While in Vienna Egon was awarded the Austrian 'Goldenes Verdienstzeichen der Republik Osterreich' (Golden Order of Merit of the Republic of Austria) in 1959 for his services to Jewish refugees.

Epilogue: Return To The UK

by Michelle Fink

Life Without Egon

Widowed at 58 and living in Vienna, Peggy decided that she no longer had any reason to live on the Continent and that she should return to the UK where her three sisters and their families were close by, and she was comfortable with the language and culture. She later also confided in me that it was so that I should feel less responsible for her—a typically selfless act!

She packed up the family home in Vienna, and a year after my father's death we were on our way to Cambridge to start a new chapter in her life. She had chosen Cambridge as both Amélie, who was now also widowed, and Joan, whose husband was in nursing care, lived in and around Cambridge. Joan had found a suitable small flat for her to buy in a 1960s development called Applecourt, which was in the same street as Amélie's house.

Peggy's aim was to establish herself in her new environment as an individual in her own right: "I do not want to be known as Dr Boyd's or Mrs Day's sister." Painfully aware of not being an academic in a city dominated by the university, she threw herself into a myriad of welfare activities, from helping out at the University Society for Visiting Scholars support group for families coming from overseas, to volunteering for the Red Cross. She joined the University of the Third

Age (U3A) and National Association of Decorative & Fine Arts Societies (NADFAS), where she not only attended lectures and outings, but also joined overseas trips, memorably a trip to China with U3A. She also sought out some of the charitable events run by the local Jewish community, with whom her post-war experiences were a source of great interest and respect, and who asked her to speak at their functions (she was the guest speaker at the Cambridge Holocaust Memorial Day in 2008). She soon became widely known as someone who knew how to help out and was invaluable for creating support networks.

Amélie, Joan, Helen, and Peggy at Loch Fyne in 1986, on the occasion of Amélie's 80th birthday

Within a short period of time she had established a large social network which she was constantly increasing. Still now, well in her 90s, she is continuously making new friends amongst people of all backgrounds and ages. There is always a supportive ear, useful no nonsense advice, and a table laden with food for all those she knows.

Despite breaking each hip twice, being affected by early onset osteoporosis, she was unstoppable in her physical activity. Each time she took on her rehabilitation as only someone on a mission to get up and going again could. She took to cycling all over Cambridge until I finally had to "ban" her after she had fallen off her bicycle and broken her hip for the third time, aged in her early 80s. She then continued driving, until again it was me who had to reinforce the medical advice she had been given to stop, given the state of her eyesight. But even then, after a short setback, she quickly took to the buses and walking, and continued her weekly swimming outings with her friends (10 laps of the pool, "even if I don't feel like it, it keeps me going"). Adapting to 'talking books' was also but a short process.

The most admirable thing about Peggy has always been her altruistic and positive outlook on life. She has always lived to help others. Her glass is always half full, and the only regret she ever expressed was that she no longer had Egon by her side. She envies elderly couples walking down the street hand in hand. More lately she also has been known to share the frustration of her badly failing eyesight—but never without following on by counting her blessings and taking delight in all the good things in life.

When looking back, her favourite way to describe her life is:

"I have had a good run for my money."

She remains an inspiration, and loves to share her past life experiences, but never ceases to live in the day.

Peggy walking on the Gog Magog hills outside Cambridge, 2004